Processing
the plan of God through
Prayer

Processing

the plan of God through

Prayer

Mark Brazee

MBM Publications
Broken Arrow, Oklahoma

Unless otherwise indicated, all Scripture quotations are taken from the *King James Version* of the Bible.

Processing the Plan of God Through Prayer
Second Printing 2000
ISBN 0-934445-07-9
Copyright © 1998 by Mark Brazee Ministries
P.O. Box 1870
Broken Arrow, Oklahoma 74013

Published by MBM Publications
P.O. Box 1870
Broken Arrow, Oklahoma 74013

Printed in the United States of America.

Contents

Introduction

A number of years ago, Janet and I had the privilege of crossing paths with a wonderful man of prayer by the name of Phil Halverson. Even though I was a serious student of the Word and did what I considered a normal amount of praying, I saw something in this man I longed to see in my own life. He not only spent time in prayer; prayer seemed to be his life.

On a few occasions, we had the honor of being with Brother Halverson and his wife, Fern, as they went into the throne room of God and took care of "future business." We listened as Brother Halverson prayed in other tongues and then as names, places, and events came forth in English. We realized he was praying about things that were yet to come.

We saw that it was not only possible but *necessary* for someone to tap into the future through the avenue of prayer and work with God concerning His plans on the Earth.

Shortly after this experience in prayer with Brother Halverson, God also divinely connected us with Reggie Scarborough, a pastor in Lakeland, Florida. The first thing I noticed in this man was his keen sensitivity to the Spirit of God.

As I spent time with Pastor Scarborough, I found the key to his ability to hear from the Spirit of God and the source of his ability to supernaturally pastor a supernatural church. I saw the same element in his life that I had seen in Brother Halverson's. Prayer—communion with God—is the key to locating and doing the plan of God.

In fellowshipping with Pastor Scarborough, he once relayed a statement God had made to him concerning prayer. He said, *"Prayer processes the plan of God."*

With his gracious permission, I have taken what the Lord spoke to him, and made it the title of this book.

These two men have made wonderful deposits into my life—deposits that have changed my life in the area of prayer. As my prayer life increased, not only was our ministry affected, but God's plans for every area of our lives were more effectively brought forth.

I trust and believe that through the pages of this book God will take that which has been imparted to my life and pass those wonderful deposits into yours. In turn, you will be enabled to reach out into the future through the avenue of prayer and, with the help of the Holy Ghost, join in a business venture with God— processing His plans on Earth!

Mark C. Brazee

Chapter 1
Doing Business With God

Throughout history, there have been many revivals or times of God manifesting His power and presence among mankind. These times and seasons of God's glory have been for the purpose of bringing forth His plans on the Earth.

Every time, without fail, as God prepares for one of these outpourings, there first comes from heaven a cry of the Spirit. As this generation is rapidly approaching its destiny—the greatest move of God this planet has ever seen or experienced—the cry of God's Spirit is going forth again.

It is the same cry that has brought forth every move of God since the beginning—*the call to pray*. It is the call for God's people to join hands in partnership with Him, doing what we can, which enables God to do what He can. *Prayer is always the catalyst which brings forth God's ability on Earth.*

As we approach this subject, it will not be simply as a religious activity with no real purpose. Instead, we will be doing business with God—doing our part to bring forth His final plans on Earth.

Praying in the River

There is a Churchwide unction on the Body of Christ to pray in these last days. What does that mean for us in the Church today? The Word of God says in Hebrews 10:5, "...a body hast thou prepared me." That verse has a twofold meaning to us in the Church. First, God prepared a physical body for Jesus to use while on the

1

Earth; second, God prepared a spiritual Body for Jesus to flow through on the Earth—and that is the Church, every born-again believer. Ephesians 1:22,23 tells us when Jesus went to the Father's right hand, God "...gave him to be the head over all things to the church, which is his body...." When Jesus came to Earth and "was made flesh and dwelt among us" (John 1:14), He was the only "body of Christ" that existed on the Earth at that time.

Since Jesus' death, burial, and resurrection, His "body" has changed. He is now the Head, and the Church is His Body down here on Earth. Today, *we* are the "Body of Christ."

Jesus is our example, and the things that affected the body of Christ then will most likely be the same things to affect the Body of Christ today. We need to look to Him to see what the Body of Christ should be doing in these last days.

For 30 years, Jesus walked and talked as a man on the Earth. During those 30 years, He didn't perform any miracles or heal multitudes. When He was 12 years old, His parents found Him in the Temple asking questions and learning. Jesus spent 30 years searching the Scriptures finding Himself. He did not have a major ministry until that time, but He did have a major job to do. He had not yet stepped into the fullness of His purpose for being on this Earth—the fullness of His calling.

Then, in Luke 3, we see Jesus about to enter into the fullness of His ministry. Where did God lead Him? To a river. Why a river? A river is a picture of a move of the Holy Ghost (John 7:37-39). God led Jesus to a river to be baptized, as we see in verses 21-23:

LUKE 3:21-23
21 Now when all the people were baptized, it came to pass, that Jesus also being baptized, and praying, the heaven was opened,
22 And the Holy Ghost descended in a bodily shape like a dove upon him, and a voice came from heaven, which said, Thou art my beloved Son; in thee I am well pleased.
23 And Jesus himself began to be about thirty years of age....

We see two things working together: the body of Christ in the river, and the body of Christ praying. *The New King James Version* says, "...Jesus also was baptized; and while He prayed, the heaven was opened." *Notice the heaven opened over the earthly body of Christ praying in the river.* When heaven opened, the Spirit of God, the anointing without measure, came upon "the body of Christ" (Luke 4:18; John 1:33). In the next three and a half years, He wrought more miracles than His disciples could record (John 21:25)!

The Church has stepped into the river of God's Spirit, and now it's time to get heaven opened. How do we do that? Through prayer! When heaven opens, it will change the Church, and when the Church changes, it will change the world!

Now that the Church or Body has stepped into the river of God's Spirit, as we learn to cooperate with the Spirit and mix that with prayer, we will step into the fullness of our purpose for being on this Earth—the rain and the harvest.

I grew up in a church where prayer was not a subject often discussed. We had a few religious prayers, but that was about the extent of it. It wasn't until years later that I began to realize the importance of prayer.

When I attended Bible school, I heard the word of faith message, which virtually changed my life. It was then that I began to study the Bible. I loved studying the Bible, and I spent extensive time doing it. Through the years, I developed good study habits, yet I had never personally taken time to develop an equally strong prayer life.

I began to see that our walk with God will never go further than our prayer life, and our prayer life will never go further than our Word level. When it comes to believing God, our faith will rise to, but never beyond, the level of our words. Similarly, our walk with God will rise to, but never go beyond, our prayer life. It is all connected. Our prayer life is directly affected by our Word life, and our Word life is directly affected by our prayer life. (John 15:7,8). Therefore, to be a person of the Word, it is vitally important to be a person of prayer.

God Is Limited by Our Prayer Life

I heard a statement from a well-known minister years ago, and it has stayed with me. Quoting John Wesley, this minister said, "It seems God is limited by our prayer life. God can do nothing for mankind unless someone asks Him."

Someone will say, "You can't limit God!"

The children of Israel limited God. Psalm 78:41 says, "Yea, they turned back and tempted God, and limited the Holy One of Israel." If the children of Israel limited God, don't you suppose it is possible for us to limit Him? It *is* possible to limit God. It *is* possible for God's will *not* to come to pass.

"How can that be?" someone will ask.

God is not willing that any should perish, but that all should come to repentance (2 Peter 3:9), yet people die and go to hell every day. People limit God by not stepping into His plan for their lives.

According to John Wesley, God can do *nothing* for mankind unless someone asks Him. That statement blows apart the thinking of most theologians. They think that a sovereign God can do anything He wants to, and if something doesn't happen, it is because God didn't want it to happen. But when a man like John Wesley, who knew God and took revival everywhere he went, said, "God can do nothing for mankind unless someone asks Him," we had better look a little closer to find the truth in that statement.

I began to study along these lines in the Bible—remember, our prayer life will never go any further than our Word life. As I went through the Word, I noticed how many times God told us to *ask*. Zechariah 10:1 says, "*Ask* ye of the Lord rain in the time of the latter rain; so the Lord shall make bright clouds, and give them showers of rain, to every one grass in the field."

If God wants rain, why doesn't He cause it to rain? Again, in Psalm 2:8, He says we have to *ask*: "*Ask* of me, and I shall give thee the heathen for thine inheritance, and the uttermost parts of the earth for thy possession."

Some will argue, "If God wants to reach the nations and the heathen, why does He say, 'Ask'? Why doesn't He just do it? After all, He's God."

Notice what Jesus Himself said in verses 37 and 38 of the following reference.

MATTHEW 9:35-38
35 And Jesus went about all the cities and villages, teaching in their synagogues, and preaching the gospel of the kingdom, and healing every sickness and every disease among the people.

36 But when he saw the multitudes, he was moved with compassion on them, because they fainted, and were scattered abroad, as sheep having no shepherd.
37 Then saith he unto his disciples, The harvest truly is plenteous, but the labourers are few;
38 Pray ye therefore the Lord of the harvest, that he will send forth labourers into his harvest.

We were ministering along these lines in another country a few years ago. After the service, one of the missionaries came to me and said, "I finally got it!"

"Got what?" I asked.

He explained, "I have been writing letters to everyone I can think of to tell them I need laborers and to please send anyone who can come help. I finally realized I've been talking to the wrong persons! I learned today that if I want laborers, I need to talk to the Lord of the harvest and ask *Him* to send laborers."

Jesus said the harvest is plenteous and the laborers are few, but we still have to ask the Lord of the harvest to send laborers into His harvest fields.

God Said, "Ask"

I have noticed throughout the Bible, if God wants something done He tells us to ask for it. "...Ye have not, because ye *ask* not" (James 4:2). "...*Ask,* and ye shall receive, that your joy may be full" (John 16:24). "And all things, whatsoever ye shall *ask* in prayer, believing, ye shall receive" (Matthew 21:22). "And whatsoever ye shall *ask* in my name, that will I do, that the Father may be glorified in the Son" (John 14:13). "If ye abide in me, and my words abide in you, ye shall *ask* what ye will, and it shall be done unto you" (John 15:7).

In the sixth chapter of Matthew, Jesus gave his disciples instructions concerning prayer. He said, "Don't be like the hypocrites who want to be seen so people can talk about how 'pretty' their prayers sound." Then He warned, "Don't be like the heathen, who think they will be heard for their *much* speaking" (verses 5 and 7, author's paraphrase).

In other words, they think if they pray long enough, loud enough, and hard enough and gather enough people to pray with them, *then* God will hear them. But Jesus said that is the way heathen pray.

So in these verses Jesus told His disciples how *not* to pray. In the next verse, He said, "Be not ye therefore like unto them: for your Father knoweth what things ye have need of, before ye ask him" (verse 8). God knows what we need before we even go to Him in prayer.

"If God knows what we need before we ask, we shouldn't have to bother asking Him, right?"

Matthew 7 helps answer that question.

MATTHEW 7:7-11
7 ASK, and it shall be given you; seek, and ye shall find; knock, and it shall be opened unto you:
8 For every one that ASKETH receiveth; and he that seeketh findeth; and to him that knocketh it shall be opened.
9 Or what man is there of you, whom if his son ASK bread, will he give him a stone?
10 Or if he ASK a fish, will he give him a serpent?
11 If ye then, being evil, know how to give good gifts unto your children, how much more shall your Father which is in heaven give good things to them that ASK him?

One chapter earlier, Jesus said the Father knows what we need before we ask; then in the next chapter He told us to ask anyway! Let's think about that for a minute. If God is that big, strong, and powerful (and He is), and He knows what we need before we ask, yet all through the Scriptures He still tells us to ask, we had better be asking Him. And when we ask God for anything, we should be expecting an answer, because God doesn't answer our requests, "Yes, no, or maybe later."

God Always Says, "Yes"

Shortly after I was born again, I asked some fellow believers why I wasn't receiving answers to my prayers. They told me, "God always answers prayer, but sometimes it's yes, and sometimes it's no." I heard another preacher say, "Sometimes God in His wisdom does not answer our prayers." No, God's wisdom doesn't lie. God's wisdom doesn't violate His Word. God's Word is His wisdom, and His Word always says yes. "For all the promises of God in him are yea, and in him Amen..." (2 Corinthians 1:20).

If we know how to pray, God will always say yes. If we pray in line with His Word and His will, which are the same, we will always receive the answer we desire. In fact, we shouldn't even pray without receiving a yes answer. If we will always go to the Scriptures first and find out what God said, we will always have the desired results. God will always answer, but the asking part is up to us.

When I found that in the Scriptures, I decided to do a lot more asking. Since then, I have been asking for the rain, the nations, the heathen—for anything God wants.

When we start asking God to move on the Earth, we are giving Him a legal invitation to bring His will to pass. Even though there are things God wants to do—things He said would happen—it takes someone going to Him in prayer and asking Him to bring those things to pass.

God is a just God. Everything He does, He does legally. Through the plan of redemption, God put prayer on a legal basis for us. Now it's our job to find out what God wants to do and give Him a legal invitation to move on this Earth and bring His will, plan, and purposes to pass.

Praying God's Will

I began to search the Scriptures along the lines of prayer, and one thing I noticed is that Earth has to do something before heaven can respond. In Matthew 6, we find Jesus teaching His disciples what is commonly called "The Lord's Prayer." Jesus' disciples had asked Him how to pray, and in this prayer Jesus gave them a demonstration or "model" of how to pray in the interim time when the Old Covenant was going out and the New Covenant was coming in. Jesus said:

> **MATTHEW 6:9,10**
> **9 After this manner therefore pray ye: Our Father which art in heaven, Hallowed be thy name.**
> **10 Thy kingdom come. THY WILL BE DONE IN EARTH, AS IT IS IN HEAVEN.**

Jesus said to pray God's will be done in the Earth as it is in heaven. God's will is already done in heaven— there is no resistance there. But to accomplish God's will on Earth, Jesus said someone has to pray. God's will on Earth won't be done simply because God wants it to be done. God's will on Earth will only be done if someone asks Him to do it.

All through the Bible, even though God wanted something done, it took prayer; it took someone asking

Him to bring it to pass. We find this to be true in
Daniel 9.

> **DANIEL 9:1,2**
> **1 In the first year of Darius the son of Ahasuerus,
> of the seed of the Medes, which was made king
> over the realm of the Chaldeans;
> 2 In the first year of his reign I Daniel
> understood by books the number of the years,
> whereof the word of the Lord came to Jeremiah
> the prophet, that he would accomplish seventy
> years in the desolations of Jerusalem.**

In other words, Daniel was reading the Book of
Jeremiah—the passage we know as Jeremiah 25:11-
14—and he found where Jeremiah prophesied by the
Holy Ghost about the 70-year period and the events
surrounding it.

At that point, Daniel realized where the Jews, as a
nation, were in time. According to the Scriptures—God's
written Word, God's plan and will—there were things
that should be taking place on the Earth. These things
had not happened, were not happening, and it did not
look as if they were ever going to happen.

What did Daniel do? Verse 3 says, "And I set my face
unto the Lord God, to seek by prayer and supplications,
with fasting, and sackcloth, and ashes." The Bible says
he *set himself to pray.* Daniel set himself to pray about
what God wanted to do in the Earth. That is a good
example for us to follow. If it worked under the Old
Covenant, we who live under the New Covenant ought
to search the Scriptures to find what God wants to do
today and go to Him with it in prayer.

Put God in Remembrance

In Genesis 15, we find another example where
prayer was necessary to bring the will of God to pass.

GENESIS 15:13,14
13 And he said unto Abram, Know of a surety that thy seed shall be a stranger in a land that is not theirs, and shall serve them; and they shall afflict them FOUR HUNDRED YEARS;
14 And also that nation, whom they shall serve, will I judge: and afterward shall they come out with great substance.

God told Abram ahead of time that Israel would go into bondage in Egypt. God told Abram what would happen, how long it would last, and how the children of Israel would finally come out of it. God said all these things would happen, but in Exodus 2, the Bible said the children of Israel had to "cry out" or pray before God sent Moses to deliver His people and bring His will to pass.

EXODUS 2:23,24
23 And it came to pass in process of time, that the king of Egypt died: and the children of Israel sighed by reason of the bondage, and THEY CRIED, and their cry came up unto God by reason of the bondage.
24 And God heard their groaning, and GOD REMEMBERED HIS COVENANT with Abraham, with Isaac, and with Jacob.

We need to understand that when God's people cried out to Him and He remembered His covenant, it does not mean God forgot. No, God did not forget. Isaiah 43 makes these things clearer.

ISAIAH 43:25,26
25 I, even I, am he that BLOTTETH OUT THY TRANSGRESSIONS for mine own sake, and will not remember thy sins.
26 PUT ME IN REMEMBRANCE: let us plead together: declare thou, that thou mayest be justified.

In verse 25, God is referring to the New Covenant.
In the Old Covenant, He covered our sins; in the New
Covenant, He washed them away. So we know this
applies to us today as much as to Israel under the Old
Covenant.

Then, in verse 26, God said, "Put me in remembrance." In other words, He said it, and now we have to
put Him in remembrance. What are we going to put
someone in remembrance about? Usually about
something they said. God is teaching us some things
about prayer. I've noticed that most of the church prays
the *problem*; we ought to be praying the *answer*.

I like what E. W. Kenyon said about prayer: "Prayer
should be God looking down to Earth and seeing a
mirror reflecting His Word back at Him."

For example, prayer should be, "Father, I thank You
that You said..." Prayer should not be, "Lord, You know
how bad I have it..." Prayer should not be reminding
God how bad our problems are; it should be reminding
God what He *said* about our problems.

Notice there is a second part to verse 26.

ISAIAH 43:26
**26 Put me in remembrance: LET US PLEAD
TOGETHER: declare thou, that thou mayest be
justified.**

The word "together" is an important key. If we are
going to plead together with someone, what do you
suppose we might be pleading? Probably the same thing
they are pleading. What we need to be doing is pleading
together with God. When we are reminding God of what
He said, we are pleading together with Him. God
already said in First Peter 2:24, "...by whose stripes ye
were healed." And when we go to Him and say, "God,

You said in Your Word by Jesus' stripes I am already healed," we are pleading together with God.

We could go to God and say, "I feel just awful. And God, You know what the doctors have said about my condition." But God says, "Yes, I know all that, but put Me in remembrance. Don't plead *against* Me; plead *with* Me."

Prayer should be, "Father, I come before You in Jesus' Name. I thank You for the blood of Jesus that made a way for me to come boldly before the throne of grace to obtain mercy and find grace to help in time of need. Dear Father, I have needs in my life, but I thank You, because You said You supply all my need according to Your riches in glory by Christ Jesus. I thank You I have been redeemed from the curse of poverty. I thank You the blessings of Abraham are overtaking me. I thank You that Mark 11:23 says I can have what I say. I say I am healed, whole, and prosperous. I say no weapon formed against me can prosper. I thank You that You said..."

That is prayer. It is not the only kind of prayer, but it is one kind. We ought to be pleading together with God—*saying the same thing God said in His Word.*

The last part of verse 26 says:

ISAIAH 43:26
26 Put me in remembrance: let us plead together: DECLARE THOU, THAT THOU MAYEST BE JUSTIFIED.

The word "justified" is defined "to be proven or shown to be just, right, or reasonable." Putting God in remembrance, pleading together, and declaring are all ways of verbalizing things. How are we going to verbalize? With words. If we are to declare or say something, we should be saying something so we can be proven or shown to be right.

If you need to be made right in your body, start saying it. If it is your finances, start saying something about your finances. Start saying what God said—start pleading together with God. Verse 26 does not say, "Plead with Me or beg Me"; it says, *"Plead together* with Me." God is the One who said, "Put Me in remembrance." He said to put Him in remembrance of His covenant promises.

God's "Remembrancers"

If we do our part, God is ready to do His; He is just waiting to be reminded. God gave us an example to follow in Isaiah 62. In verse 6, Isaiah said, "I have set watchmen upon thy walls, O Jerusalem, which shall never hold their peace day nor night: ye that make mention of the Lord, keep not silence." Next to that verse in the *King James Version* there is a marginal note which reads, "...ye that are the Lord's *remembrancers*...." To whom is Isaiah referring? Those who pray.

We could say, "I have set watchmen upon thy walls, O Jerusalem, which shall never hold their peace day nor night: *ye who are the Lord's remembrancers*, keep not silence." "Prayers" are God's remembrancers. They remind God of what He said and of what He wants to do.

Isaiah continued in verse 7, "And give him no rest, till he establish, and till he make Jerusalem a praise in the earth."

People say, "I don't want to bother God with anything." But the Bible says, "Give Him no silence and give Him no rest."

Of course, this Scripture is dealing with Zion and a particular situation, but Zion is a type of the Church. (See Hebrews 12:22,23.) So what Isaiah spoke in the Old Testament still pertains to the Church today and will work for us the same as it worked for them. We are the Lord's remembrancers, and we should not give Him any rest until the fruit of our prayers—what is supposed to come forth—manifests.

That is what the children of Israel did. After 430 years, the children of Israel had grown tired of their bondage. They began to cry out to God and put Him in remembrance of what He had said in Genesis 15:13.

At that point, God spoke to Moses on the backside of the desert, called him, equipped him with signs and wonders, and sent him to Egypt to lead Israel into God's plan of freedom. The Israelites were brought out of the bondage of Egypt with great substance, just as God had promised. But God did not move until someone cried out. His will did not come to pass until someone prayed!

Elijah the Rain Prophet

The Old Testament prophet Elijah is an example of someone who prayed in order to bring God's will to pass in the Earth. In the Book of First Kings, we see that Elijah prayed, and the rain stopped for three and a half years. He prayed again, and the rain began to fall. Elijah knew something about prayer in connection with the rain.

1 KINGS 17:1
1 And Elijah the Tishbite, who was of the inhabitants of Gilead, said unto Ahab, As the Lord God of Israel liveth, BEFORE WHOM I STAND, there shall not be dew nor rain these years, but according to my word.

One thing we see from this verse is the strength of Elijah's ministry. Elijah took time to stand before God. How did he stand before God? In prayer. Elijah was a man of prayer and that is why God was able to use him so mightily.

James makes reference to Elijah's prayer life in James 5:17,18:

> 17 Elias was a man subject to like passions as we are, and HE PRAYED EARNESTLY that it might not rain: and it rained not on the earth by the space of three years and six months.
> 18 And HE PRAYED AGAIN, and the heaven gave rain, and the earth brought forth her fruit.

Elijah prayed and received *physical* rain. When we pray, we will receive *spiritual* rain. Why is rain so important? Because rain is what will bring in the harvest the Lord is waiting for before Jesus returns. We can see there is a direct correlation between prayer and the rain.

Referring to the Old Testament, the Lord spoke to Elijah again about the rain.

> 1 KINGS 18:1
> 1 And it came to pass after many days, that THE WORD OF THE LORD CAME TO ELIJAH in the third year, saying, Go, shew thyself unto Ahab; and I will send rain upon the earth.

Elijah heard from heaven in a time of prayer. He received directions from God on what to do next. Elijah went to find Obadiah, King Ahab's right-hand man, to give him the message that rain was coming. Remember, there had been no rain for three and a half years at this point. There was a great drought and a famine in the land.

Ahab was out looking for water so he might save his animals, and the last person he wanted to see was the one who had brought about the drought and famine! When Ahab finally came to Elijah, he said, "...Art thou he that troubleth Israel?" (1 Kings 18:17).

Elijah threw the accusation right back at Ahab, saying, "...I have not troubled Israel; but thou, and thy father's house, in that ye have forsaken the commandments of the Lord, and thou hast followed Baalim" (verse 18).

Elijah instructed Ahab to gather all the false prophets—the 450 prophets of Baal and the 400 prophets who sat at Jezebel's table—to come together for a showdown. All day the false prophets tried to call down fire on their sacrifice. But fire doesn't fall from a dead god. Finally, Elijah stepped up, rebuilt the altar, drenched the sacrifice in water, and prayed aloud to God.

In verse 38 we read, "Then the fire of the Lord fell, and consumed the burnt sacrifice, and the wood, and the stones, and the dust, and licked up the water that was in the trench." All the people shouted, "The Lord He is God! The Lord He is God!" One dose of fire changed the entire nation!

Elijah then had all the false prophets killed. In verse 41, he said to Ahab, "...Get thee up, eat and drink; for there is a sound of abundance of rain."

In verse 1, God told Elijah He was going to send rain, and in verse 41, Elijah heard the rain coming. But even though God said the rain was coming, and even though Elijah heard the rain, *Elijah still had to pray the rain through to the Earth!*

Prayer Precedes a Move of God

I am convinced God will not do anything on the Earth unless someone asks Him to do it. To get results in prayer, we ought to know what to pray for. However, sometimes we may not know enough about a situation to ask God to move, and that is a weakness or an infirmity.

That is why it is so important to pray in the Holy Ghost or in other tongues. When we pray in other tongues, we are asking God to do things we don't even know about, and He will help us to pray out the perfect will of God.

Romans 8:26 says, "Likewise the Spirit also helpeth our infirmities: for we know not what we should pray for as we ought: but the Spirit itself maketh intercession for us with groanings which cannot be uttered."

In Acts 1, Jesus gave His disciples specific directions about what would happen when the Holy Ghost was poured out. But He also said, "Before you go, WAIT."

ACTS 1:8
8 But YE SHALL RECEIVE POWER, AFTER THAT THE HOLY GHOST IS COME UPON YOU: and ye shall be witnesses unto me both in Jerusalem, and in all Judaea, and in Samaria, and unto the uttermost part of the earth.

The disciples didn't know what to expect—they had never seen this power that was coming. They just followed Jesus' instructions. The disciples knew they were supposed to wait for an enduement of power that would change their lives.

One of the most dramatic changes was in Peter. The power changed Peter—a man who denied Jesus three times in one night and was too timid to witness to a little girl—into a bold preacher who got 3000 people saved in his first altar call and 5000 in his second.

That power was the spark needed to ignite all the fuel or Word the disciples had received. They had been at Jesus' feet hearing the Word for three and a half years, but they still didn't have boldness to witness. So Jesus said, "Wait in the Upper Room and I'll give you something to ignite that fuel and change your lives." Jesus didn't say, "You will *go* witness," He said, "You will *be* a witness."

Jesus gave the disciples the instructions, and history tells us that 120 gathered in the Upper Room for 10 days before the Day of Pentecost arrived. Do you know what the 120 believers did for those 10 days? The Bible says, "These all continued with one accord in *prayer* and *supplication...*" (Acts 1:14).

Jesus told the disciples what He wanted to happen, but it took 10 days of prayer and supplication to pray through this mighty move of God. They knew there was a move coming, but again, *God's plan had to be processed through prayer.*

In Acts 2, the outpouring came. They prayed until the power of God fell!

ACTS 2:1-4
1 And when the day of Pentecost was fully come, they were all with one accord in one place.
2 And suddenly there came a sound from heaven as of a rushing mighty wind, and it filled all the house where they were sitting.
3 And there appeared unto them cloven tongues like as of fire, and it sat upon each of them.
4 And they were all filled with the Holy Ghost, and began to speak with other tongues, as the Spirit gave them utterance.

The fullness of the Spirit came, and the 120 all enjoyed the manifested presence of God. They had been hiding in the Upper Room, but after they were endued with power, they headed into the streets of Jerusalem. Peter preached the first message there, and 3000 people were saved. This outpouring of power brought about some radical changes! The Early Church had come through the doorway. The initial outpouring had come, and they were all baptized in the Holy Ghost. The early rain started to fall—but they had to keep moving through the doorway. The next thing we see is Peter and John going to the Temple *at the hour of prayer*. In Acts 3, Peter and John arrived at the gate called Beautiful where a lame man was laid daily to ask alms.

> **ACTS 3:4-8**
> **4 And Peter, fastening his eyes upon him with John, said, Look on us.**
> **5 And he gave heed unto them, expecting to receive something of them.**
> **6 Then Peter said, Silver and gold have I none; but such as I have give I thee: In the name of Jesus Christ of Nazareth rise up and walk.**
> **7 And he took him by the right hand, and lifted him up: and immediately his feet and ankle bones received strength.**
> **8 And he leaping up stood, and walked, and entered with them into the temple, walking, and leaping, and praising God.**

Peter preached a message, and this time 5000 people were saved. Then, in Acts 4, Peter and John were threatened by the authorities and commanded not to preach and teach in the name of Jesus.

> **ACTS 4:23,24**
> **23 And being let go, they went to their own company, and reported all that the chief priests and elders had said unto them.**
> **24 And when they heard that, they lifted up their voice to God with one accord, and said, Lord, thou art God, which hast made heaven, and earth, and the sea, and all that in them is.**

Peter and John returned to their own company and prayed. In the last part of their prayer they prayed, "And now, Lord, behold their threatenings: and grant unto thy servants, that with all boldness they may speak thy word, by stretching forth thine hand to heal; and that signs and wonders may be done by the name of thy holy child Jesus" (verses 29,30).

What did they do? The disciples knew it was time for an increase in the move of the Holy Ghost, so they prayed again. They prayed for boldness, healing, and signs and wonders. And in Acts 5:12, "...by the hands of the apostles were many signs and wonders wrought among the people...."

Each time the Church prayed, they prayed through another move of God. They went to the Upper Room and prayed through the early rain. Then they switched gears and prayed through another aspect of the move of God which brought healings, and signs and wonders. Whenever it was time for a change, the Church prayed.

In Acts 13, it was time for a great missionary thrust to the nations.

> **ACTS 13:1-3**
> **1 Now there were in the church that was at Antioch certain prophets and teachers; as Barnabas, and Simeon that was called Niger, and Lucius of Cyrene, and Manaen, which had been brought up with Herod the tetrarch, and Saul.**
> **2 As they ministered to the Lord, and fasted, the Holy Ghost said, Separate me Barnabas and Saul for the work whereunto I have called them.**
> **3 And when they had FASTED and PRAYED, and laid their hands on them, they sent them away.**

In a time of prayer, Paul and Barnabas were separated to the purpose for which they were born on the Earth, and they stepped out to take the Gospel to the entire Gentile world.

Prayer causes things to happen! Anytime God wanted to do something, He stirred the Church to pray. In Acts 12, Herod had put Peter in prison and planned to behead him after Easter. What happened? Acts 12:5 says, "...prayer was made *without ceasing* of the church unto God for him." The margin of my Bible says, "instant and earnest prayer."

The Church went to prayer, and while they were praying, an angel walked into the prison and delivered Peter! The angel led him right out the door, then disappeared. Peter went on to finish his course, but it would not have happened without prayer.

Then, in Acts 16, Paul and Silas were on a missionary journey. They had been beaten and put into the inner prison with their feet fastened in stocks. Did they murmur and complain about their situation? No. The Bible says they *prayed!*

> **ACTS 16:25,26**
> **25 And at midnight Paul and Silas PRAYED, and SANG PRAISES unto God: and the prisoners heard them.**
> **26 And suddenly there was a great earthquake, so that the foundations of the prison were shaken: and immediately all the doors were opened, and every one's bands were loosed.**

Why was there "suddenly" a great earthquake? Because Paul and Silas prayed and sang praises.

The Early Church knew the importance of prayer in bringing God's will to pass in the Earth. We read in Acts 6, that those who were God's ministers were so busy waiting on tables and tending to the needs of the people, they didn't have time to do what they should have been doing—which was praying and studying the Word.

ACTS 6:2-4
2 Then the twelve called the multitude of the
disciples unto them, and said, It is not reason that
we should leave the word of God, and serve tables.
3 Wherefore, brethren, look ye out among you
seven men of honest report, full of the Holy Ghost
and wisdom, whom we may appoint over this
business.
4 But WE WILL GIVE OURSELVES CONTIN-
UALLY TO PRAYER, and to the ministry of the
word.

What happened? The Church began to explode! The
ministry of helps was raised up, the ministers were able
to do their jobs, believers moved into their proper
positions—and it was all related to prayer. Prayer is
vital to the plan of God. There are things God wants to
accomplish—things He has said He is going to do—but it
still takes someone to pray to bring those things to pass.

Standing in the Gap

I remember a story of a young woman who had been
attacked with sickness in her body. She was a college
student at the time, and the doctors could not seem to
pinpoint what was wrong with her. She was born again
and baptized in the Holy Ghost, but for some reason she
was not able to receive her healing and kept getting
worse. A friend of mine who knew of the situation told
me he went home from work and told his wife they
needed to pray for the young woman.

They hit their knees and prayed for at least two
hours until the burden to pray for her finally lifted. A
few days later, my friend and his wife received word
that the very moment they started to pray, the young
woman's condition began to improve, and to this day
she is perfectly well. The doctors never could explain it.

God wanted her healed so badly, He moved upon someone else to hook up to heaven and pray!

If God had wanted her healed so badly, why didn't He just reach down and heal her? Because God needed someone to *ask* Him to do it. Ezekiel 22:30 says, "And I sought for a man among them, that should make up the hedge, and stand in the gap before me for the land, that I should not destroy it: but I found none." God is looking for someone who will ask—someone who will stand in the gap and make up the hedge!

We were in a church service years ago where the minister addressed the congregation about Watergate and former President Richard Nixon. He said to the crowd, "The President really blew it. He really sold us out." The people agreed with him, and before long they almost had a lynch mob forming in the church. The minister kept on, feeding the congregation enough rope to tie their own "noose."

He finally stopped and said, "It is all *our* fault if we weren't praying!" The place grew quiet in a hurry. If the Church would pray, God would change things. That is why the apostle Paul said by the Spirit in First Timothy 2:1,2 to pray for those in authority, "...that we may lead a quiet and peaceable life in all godliness and honesty."

God desires to carry out His will in the Earth. He is simply looking for someone to ask Him to do it.

Understanding of the Times

The Church has a job to do in these last days. We are living in the time of the greatest outpouring of the Spirit of God, and there are things God wants and needs to have happen to bring His plans to pass. When we understand the times in which we are living, we will know what it is God wants to do, and we will be quick to pray and bring His will to pass in the Earth.

We read in First Chronicles 12:32, "And of the children of Issachar, which were men that had *understanding of the times,* to know what Israel ought to do...."

The Bible calls the children of Issachar "men that had understanding of the times." When these men understood the times, they knew what to do. We need to understand there are certain events for which God has set or appointed times.

Of course, when it comes to salvation, the baptism of the Holy Ghost, divine healing, prosperity—the blessings of God that belong to us because of the death, burial, and resurrection of Jesus—there is no set time. Those things have already been bought and paid for by the precious blood of the Lord Jesus. But when we refer to national events, moves of God, revivals, and outpourings, there are set times or seasons for them to take place.

There was an *appointed* time for Jesus to be born. Galatians 4:4 says, "But when the fulness of the time was come, God sent forth his Son...." There was an *appointed* time for Jesus to go to the cross. There was an *appointed* time for Jesus to be raised from the dead. There was an *appointed* time for the Holy Spirit to be poured out. Acts 2:1 says, "And when the day of Pentecost was *fully come,* they were all with one accord in one place."

It was no coincidence that the Holy Spirit was poured out on the Day of Pentecost. That day had significance, because Pentecost was the Feast of Harvest. The outpouring of the Holy Ghost is for harvest! It is for us to be endued with power to be witnesses for Jesus.

In the Old Testament Book of Esther, God had an appointed time to save an entire nation. God needed to deliver the Jews from destruction. During the reign of King Ahasuerus, deceitful men in the country were conspiring to annihilate the Jews. Esther was also a Jew, and because of her position as queen, she had access to the king. Esther's cousin Mordecai came to her and exposed the plans of the men who wanted to destroy the Jews. He warned:

> **ESTHER 4:14**
> **14 For if thou altogether holdest thy peace at this time, then shall there enlargement and deliverance arise to the Jews from another place; but thou and thy father's house shall be destroyed: and who knoweth whether thou art come to the kingdom FOR SUCH A TIME AS THIS?**

Esther was able to alert the king and bring deliverance to the entire Jewish nation. God could have easily raised up someone else to accomplish His plans, but Esther was in the right place at the right time.

I like what Mordecai told Esther: "For if thou altogether holdest thy peace at this time, then shall there enlargement and deliverance arise to the Jews from *another* place...." Thank God, *the whole kingdom of God does not depend on one person.* God will get the job done if He has to raise someone else up to do it. Mordecai went on to say, "...who knoweth whether thou art come to the kingdom *for such a time as this?*"

That is where the Church is right now. We have come to the kingdom *for such a time as this!* We in the Church do not fully realize the destiny that is on our generation. This is the time of the greatest outpouring in the history of the Earth. It is a time when decisions are critical, and doing the will of God is crucial.

All through history, there have been appointed times for things, and these last days are no different. God always does things in times; and once we understand the times in which we are living, we will know our responsibility and what we should do.

What should the Church do? *Pray!* Prayer causes situations and circumstances to change and brings God's will to pass in the Earth.

Prayer Produces the Power of God

In reading the works of famed missionary John G. Lake, I found he refers to the praying Church as the generating power of God in the Earth.

One night, Dr. Lake sat on a hill overlooking many villages in South Africa. He counted 1,100 villages and miles of land within the range of his vision. This territory represented millions of people still untouched by the Gospel of Jesus Christ.

As Dr. Lake cried out to God about what could be done to reach these people, he heard the Spirit of the Lord say, "The Church, which is His Body." Dr. Lake knew that the Church was doing everything possible in the natural to reach the people, so this phrase had to mean something else. Finally, Dr. Lake understood it: To have the will of God in the Earth, it was going to take the Church, the Body of Christ, praying the will and plan of God down to the Earth.

Dr. Lake saw that the praying Church is like a generator or dynamo that produces electricity. Power is always present, but it takes an avenue to channel that power where it is needed so it can be used. Thus, prayer is like God's divine dynamo. It produces the power to generate God's will on the Earth.

Praying the Fire Down

We were in a church not long ago where the youth group was stronger than I have seen in a long time. The group had been going strong a few years earlier, but then the youth pastor moved to another location as part of God's plan for his life. Another youth pastor took over and did a tremendous job. However, somehow in the transition the youth group lost its momentum.

Anyone who has worked with youth knows that once the fire goes out, all that remains are billows of smoke and coals that have to be stirred up again. I knew at one point the group had dwindled down to a handful of kids. At this particular service, however, I noticed there were two to three rows of youth present.

I was in the middle of my message, and all of a sudden the power of God fell and hit those young people! They started leaping out of their chairs, shouting, dancing, and running all over the building. Then they fell out under the power of God and lay in the front of the sanctuary for the rest of the service. We held meetings at that church the entire week, and in every service similar things happened with the youth.

What had happened to cause such a change? We decided to find out, so we spoke to one of the young girls in the group. She and another girl knew the fire had burned out, and they decided they had to have the power back. They started meeting every day to pray for two to three hours. (It doesn't take thousands of people to make a change.) They were soon joined by others.

It took a few weeks, but soon these young people literally "prayed the fire down" on their youth group! The fire fell and ignited the whole youth group to pray. We started the evening meetings that week at 7 o'clock, but the youth group had been there praying since 4 o'clock every day!

It seemed all these teenagers wanted to do was pray! I heard some people say, "Well, they are just kids." No, you mark my words and watch—when the fire of God hits these "kids," you'd better get out of their way! These youth were hungry for a move of God, and their prayers produced the power of God.

If You Abide in Me

I am convinced if the Church will take her place in prayer, find out what God wants to do, and ask Him to do it, the will, plan, and purposes of God will be accomplished in the Earth.

Jesus told us in John 15:7, "If ye abide in me, and my words abide in you, ye shall ask what ye will, and it shall be done unto you." That's a strong statement. It's the kind of statement that rocks "religious boats" and kicks over "sacred cows." But if we stop and think about it, Jesus is the One who said it. Notice, however, Jesus said, "If..." He gave us two conditions: *If* ye abide in Me, and my words abide in you...*then* you will ask whatever you will. Jesus said we can ask whatever we will!

Someone says, "That's a blank check."

That's right. Jesus said if we do two things—we may ask whatever we will. God inserted a check-and-balance system so people wouldn't write "blank checks" for crazy things. God said *if* we abide in Him, walk in fellowship with Him, and have His Word abiding in us, we can ask anything we will, and it shall be done. If we walk in fellowship with God and are full of His Word, we will not ask for anything that is not in line with His will.

I have heard people say, particularly about healing, "Brother Mark, you say God wants to heal everyone, and healing belongs to everyone."

I am guilty. I have said it, and I believe it. How can I believe that to be true? Because by Jesus' stripes we *were* healed. It's not a promise; it's a fact. I know it is the will of God to *heal* everyone, just as I also know it is the will of God to *save* everyone! However, these things are sometimes conditional, meaning we have to do something to receive them.

"Well, if it's God's will, it will happen." Not necessarily. It is God's will to save everyone, but will everyone be saved? "...*whosoever* shall call on the name of the Lord shall be saved" (Acts 2:21). We have to do something about it.

It is God's will to heal everyone, but what happens? We still have to do something. If we do our part, God does His. God does not change His mind, and He does not lie. If we don't receive healing, we have not done our part.

Someone will say, "That sounds hard."

No, it's *truth*. God doesn't promise healing, purchase it for us, and then turn around and say, "In My wisdom I have decided not to heal you." Healing belongs to us, but we have to do something to get it. Salvation belongs to the world, but the world has to do something to get it. What is that? Reach out and *take it!* Faith says, "It is mine; I take it now."

People have said, "Well, I knew so-and-so, and he was a good person. He didn't get healed, so healing cannot be for everyone." We cannot base our faith walk on what someone else did or did not receive. Faith is of the heart, and we have no way of knowing what is in someone else's heart. We have to judge everything by the Word of God. The moment we start judging things on someone's experience, we are on shaky ground.

"You don't understand. He was so consecrated to God. He loved God and served Him. But he didn't get healed, and if anyone deserved to be healed, he did." The bottom line is, no one deserves it. Nothing comes from God based on our works or our deserving anything.

If the benefits of redemption were based on deserving, none of us would even go to heaven! No, the blessings of God don't come on a deserving basis; they come on a *grace* basis. Grace means "unearned favor." If God's Word abides in us, we will know what His will is in these areas.

Many times in the Church world, people only meet one of the conditions of John 15:7. Thus, they are not walking in the blessings of asking whatever they will and receiving it. There are others who meet both conditions, and they experience results. Jesus did not say, "If you abide in Me, and My words abide at home on the coffee table." No. "If you abide in Me, and you go to church every Sunday." No. "If you abide in Me, and you carry a Bible everywhere you go." No. "If you abide in Me, and you witness to everyone you meet." No.

Those are all important things, but that is not what Jesus said. He said, "If you abide in me, *and my words abide in you*, ye shall ask what ye will, and it shall be done unto you." God wants our prayers answered. That's why He said in John 16:24, "...ask, and ye shall receive, that your joy may be full." When God's Word abides in us, we won't ask for anything unscriptural.

When it comes to praying for ourselves, sometimes we pray too quickly. What we should do first is take the time to make sure we are abiding in Him, and then determine that His Word is abiding in us. How do we do that? Go to God's Word and find Scriptures that promise us what we are asking Him for.

Because the Church has not taken the time to find Scriptures to stand on, our prayer life has been somewhat weak. We have jumped right into prayer, aimlessly throwing out many different prayers and hoping God will answer at least one of them.

Mirror Reflecting God's Word

We ought to be right on target in prayer every time. If we take time to abide in Him and get His Word abiding in us, when we go to God in prayer, we will be like mirrors reflecting His Word back at Him, and that is when we will get the desired results.

The blessings and benefits of God always begin with His Word. Isaiah 5:13 says, "Therefore my people are gone into captivity, because they have no knowledge...." If captivity is the result of a lack of knowledge, freedom and fruit are the results of knowledge. We can see it throughout God's Word. Peter wrote, "Grace and peace be multiplied unto you *through the knowledge of God,* and of Jesus our Lord" (2 Peter 1:2). The first Psalm shows us the blessings of walking in the knowledge of God and the consequences of disregarding God's Word.

> **PSALM 1:1-6**
> 1 **Blessed is the man that walketh not in the counsel of the ungodly, nor standeth in the way of sinners, nor sitteth in the seat of the scornful.**
> 2 **But HIS DELIGHT IS IN THE LAW OF THE LORD; and in his law doth he meditate day and night.**
> 3 **And he shall be like a tree planted by the rivers of water, that bringeth forth his fruit in his season; his leaf also shall not wither; and whatsoever he doeth shall prosper.**
> 4 **The ungodly are not so: but are like the chaff which the wind driveth away.**
> 5 **Therefore the ungodly shall not stand in the judgment, nor sinners in the congregation of the righteous.**
> 6 **For the Lord knoweth the way of the righteous: but the way of the ungodly shall perish.**

Joshua also shows us the importance of God's Word abiding in us.

JOSHUA 1:8
8 This book of the law SHALL NOT DEPART OUT OF THY MOUTH; but THOU SHALT MEDITATE THEREIN DAY AND NIGHT, that thou mayest observe to do according to all that is written therein: for then thou shalt make thy way prosperous, and then thou shalt have good success.

Fruitfulness in prayer is greatly dependent upon God's Word dwelling in our hearts. We can see that not only the written Word, as we found in Daniel 9, but also the spoken word, as we found in Genesis 15, had to be "prayed through" to come to pass on the Earth.

Often God speaks to us through a spoken word by the Holy Ghost or in a time of prayer, but we put it on the shelf and say, "If it's God's will, it will happen." What happens when we have that kind of attitude? Nothing!

What we should say is, "God, You said it, I believe it, and that settles it!" We don't have to make it happen, but we do have to put faith behind it. How do we put faith behind it? By our words. "Declare thou, that thou mayest be justified."

We need to continually remind God of whatever He said to us. When we grab hold of God's Word, whether written or spoken, and actively remind Him of it, then His Word, will, and plan will come to pass!

Chapter 2
Praying Out the Will of God

Maria Woodworth-Etter was a woman minister mightily used by God. In her book *Acts of the Holy Ghost*, she recounts a vision where God took her to heaven. There she saw beautiful vials on a shelf. When she asked an angel who was standing nearby what was in the vials, the angel told her the vials were filled with the prayers of the saints. A special week of prayer had just taken place on Earth, and those prayers were contained in beautiful new vials lining the shelves in heaven.

Revelation 5:8 says, "And when he had taken the book, the four beasts and four and twenty elders fell down before the Lamb, having every one of them harps, and *golden vials full of odours, which are the prayers of saints.*"

Our prayers are precious to God. The Bible says heaven is filled with the prayers of the saints. Our prayers are so tangible, when they are uttered to God in faith, they go up to heaven and fill golden vials or bottles.

A grandparent may offer a prayer for his or her grandchild before going on to be with the Lord. Years later, that prayer is still contained in a vial, as God is using every opportunity to answer it and bring His will to pass. So our prayers do not fall to the Earth void; they go up as incense before God and are contained in golden vials, where He begins working on them to bring them to pass.

The Purpose of Prayer

When I understood that God—the Creator of the universe—needs someone to ask Him to move, it turned prayer from a chore into a pleasure for me. It helped me to know *why* I should pray.

Prayer is not some kind of form or ritual. Prayer is not something we do simply because God said to do it. There is much more to prayer than that. When we can understand the purpose of why we are praying, it will help us pray much more effectively and with greater fervency.

Our prayer life will affect what God is able to do on this Earth. Why? Because prayer gives God a legal invitation to do what He wants to do. Some people can simply accept the fact God is limited by our prayer life, and in order for Him to move, it takes someone asking Him.

I, on the other hand, have always wondered not only *how* things work, but *why* they work. I have ruined many mechanical items trying to figure out how they work. When I was about two years old, my parents caught me trying to take the door off the house! I wanted to figure out how the hinges worked. I have always taken apart watches, cars, and anything else I could think of, trying to understand how and why things worked.

I guess that curiosity carried over to the things of God. I wanted to know why prayer was so important. I wanted to know the purpose for prayer. I found out prayer is not talking God into doing something. It is not twisting God's arm. Prayer is not gathering enough people to pray. It is not praying loud enough or long enough. When I found out what prayer is and what prayer is for, I found the purpose for prayer. I realized prayer is doing business with God. *Prayer is finding out what God wants to do and then asking Him to do it.*

Putting Prayer on a Legal Basis

Hebrews 2 helps us build a foundation for the purpose of prayer. Paul, inspired by the Holy Ghost, wrote to the Hebrew Christians in verses 6-8:

> **HEBREWS 2:6-8**
> **6 But one in a certain place testified, saying, What is man, that thou art mindful of him? or the son of man, that thou visitest him?**
> **7 Thou madest him a little lower than the angels; thou crownedst him with glory and honour, and didst set him over the works of thy hands:**
> **8 Thou hast put all things in subjection under his feet. For in that he put all in subjection under him, he left nothing that is not put under him. But now we see not yet all things put under him.**

We find God's plan for man in these verses. God created us, crowned us with glory and honor, set us over all the works of His hands, and put everything under our feet. Dominion and authority were given to man by God.

We can see in verse 6 that Paul was referring to a previously recorded Scripture when he wrote, "But one in a certain place testified, saying, What is man, that thou art mindful of him?..." He was referring to what the psalmist wrote in Psalm 8:

> **PSALM 8:3-9**
> **3 When I consider thy heavens, the work of thy fingers, the moon and the stars, which thou hast ordained;**
> **4 What is man, that thou art mindful of him? and the son of man, that thou visitest him?**

> 5 For thou hast made him a little lower than the
> angels, and hast crowned him with glory and
> honour.
> 6 Thou madest him to have dominion over the
> works of thy hands; thou hast put all things under
> his feet:
> 7 All sheep and oxen, yea, and the beasts of the
> field;
> 8 The fowl of the air, and the fish of the sea, and
> whatsoever passeth through the paths of the seas.
> 9 O Lord our Lord, how excellent is thy name in
> all the earth!

Let's go back to the book of beginnings to see where
this is first recorded.

> **GENESIS 1:26**
> 26 And God said, Let us make man in our image,
> after our likeness: and let them have dominion
> over the fish of the sea, and over the fowl of the
> air, and over the cattle, and over all the earth, and
> over every creeping thing that creepeth upon the
> earth.

Notice God said, "Let *them* have dominion." God's
plan was not for Adam alone but for all mankind.

> **GENESIS 1:27,28**
> 27 So God created man in his own image, in the
> image of God created he him; male and female
> created he them.
> 28 And God blessed them, and God said unto them,
> Be fruitful, and multiply, and replenish the earth,
> and subdue it: and have dominion over the fish of
> the sea, and over the fowl of the air, and over
> every living thing that moveth upon the earth.

God formed man out of the dust of the Earth and
breathed His own life into him. The Bible says that man
is a "living soul" (Genesis 2:7). If we stop and think

about it, God is a Spirit, and He lives in the spirit realm. God had no need for a natural world.

Psalm 24:1 says, "The earth is the Lord's, and the fulness thereof...." It all belongs to God, but He doesn't need this natural world. What He did need, however, was fellowship.

God had angels, cherubim, seraphim, and archangels, but He wanted someone he could walk with in the cool of the day and talk with face to face. God wanted someone made in His own image and after His own likeness. He didn't want someone He would command, but someone with whom He could have fellowship. He wanted someone who would serve Him not because they had to, but because they wanted to—not a robot, but a free moral agent.

Every person has the choice to die and go to hell if they so desire. God will not force anyone into choosing Him. He won't force anyone to be baptized in the Holy Ghost or to be healed. Man has always had a choice, and he still has a choice.

Adam's Authority

God didn't need Earth, but He needed us and loved us so much He created us, created a place for us, and then gave us dominion and authority over it and everything in it. In one context, we could say that Adam was "the god of this world." Some people flinch at that terminology, but technically it's true.

Adam had all authority given to him by God. He even had dominion over the serpent who came to tempt Eve; however, he did not use that authority.

Many of the problems we have surface because we are not using our God-given authority. We are sitting back waiting for God to do something instead of using the authority He gave us. We are supposed to keep the "snakes" out of the garden, not take a seat and listen to them. If they rear their ugly heads, we are supposed to run them out. It's our garden!

In God's original plan, Adam was placed in the garden and had dominion over everything God created. God told Adam, "...Of every tree of the garden thou mayest freely eat: But of the tree of the knowledge of good and evil, thou shalt not eat of it: for in the day that thou eatest thereof thou shalt surely die" (Genesis 2:16,17).

I had always wondered why God put both trees in the garden. Why didn't He put the tree of life in the garden and the tree of knowledge of good and evil somewhere like Antarctica? Then it would have taken man 5000 years to find it, and by then no one would have wanted it anyway. Did God put both trees in the garden to test man? No. "Let no man say when he is tempted, I am tempted of God: for God cannot be tempted with evil, neither tempteth he any man" (James 1:13).

God wanted man to serve Him by choice. The only way man can be a person of choice is to be given a choice to make. God desired for man to serve Him and fellowship with Him, but if man didn't want to, there was another tree for him to choose.

Human nature went to work immediately, and Adam and Eve disobeyed God. The minute they ate of the tree, they separated themselves from God. Immediately, Adam realized he was naked. The first thing he tried to do after he sinned was cover himself with fig leaves. God came to fellowship with His man, and instead Adam hid from God.

Authority Transferred

Something else happened here in the garden. Looking again at Hebrews 2:8, the first part of the verse says, "Thou hast put all things in subjection under his feet. For in that he put all in subjection under him, he left nothing that is not put under him...." The last part of the verse reads, "...But now we see not yet all things put under him."

Something happened between the beginning and the end of verse 8. What was it? It was the fall in the garden. Technically, Adam was the god of this world. God had given Adam dominion and authority and put everything under his feet. But when Adam disobeyed God and obeyed Satan, not only did he separate himself from God, but he transferred everything God had given him to a new master!

Notice Second Corinthians 4:4: "In whom the god of this world hath blinded the minds of them which believe not, lest the light of the glorious gospel of Christ, who is the image of God, should shine unto them." Here Satan is referred to as "the god of this world." Ephesians 2:2 calls him "the prince of the power of the air."

In Luke 4, Satan came to tempt Jesus in the wilderness. Verse 5 says Satan took Jesus to a pinnacle and showed Him *all the kingdoms of the world* in a moment of time. Satan said to Jesus, "...All this power will I give thee, and the glory of them: for that is delivered unto me; and to whomsoever I will I give it" (verse 6).

Notice Satan did not say, "All this is mine"; he said, "All this *has been delivered* to me." Who delivered it to Satan? The last one to have possession of it. God had it, and He gave it to Adam. It was a gift, which means it could be passed on or given away. That is why Satan could say to Jesus, "If you will worship me, I will give all these kingdoms of the world to You." Of course, Jesus didn't take them, and Satan remains the god of this world—which is why this world is in such a mess.

Jesus wasn't going to take the old creation. He came and started a brand-new one right in the middle of the old one! "Therefore if any man be in Christ, he is a new creature: old things are passed away; behold, all things are become new" (2 Corinthians 5:17). Jesus is the first-born of a new creation and, thank God, He didn't come and reclaim the old creation. He started a new creation, and everything else is still under our feet. We may be *in* the world, but we are not *of* it. Satan is the god of this world, but we are not of this world; therefore, Satan is not god over us.

We could say it another way. God owns the Earth, but when He created Adam, He gave him a long lease on creation. When Adam disobeyed God, he "sublet" everything God had given him. If we understand these terms it will help us put things in perspective. God gave Adam what legally belonged to Him, but Adam transferred everything to Satan. In a sense, Satan received a "sublease," and everything God gave to Adam was legally transferred to Satan. Thus, Satan became the god of this world.

Someone will ask, "What does this have to do with prayer?"

God is not only holy; He is also just. When Satan's lease runs out, he is not going to be able to turn to God and say, "I was unjust, but You were, too. I cheated, but You did, too." Everything God does He does legally, and that requires *prayer*.

If God did things based on *power*, He could breathe on the Earth out of one nostril, burn it up, and start over again. He could breathe on every person, wipe out sickness and disease, and take care of everyone's needs all at the same time. God's hand is not shortened that He cannot save (Isaiah 59:1). God has the power to do anything that needs to be done. But because of His Word and His plan, God does not do things on a power basis; He does them on a legal basis.

Legal Residence

There are technically two groups of "beings" living legally on the Earth. First, there is Satan and all of his cohorts: principalities, powers, rulers of the darkness of this world, and spiritual wickedness in high places (Ephesians 6:12). Satan is the god of this world, and he lives here legally, but people haven't had a full understanding of that fact.

This means we cannot command devils to go back to the pit or try to pull down strongholds over cities. No, demons have a legal *right* to be here! It is not our job to run the demons off; it is our job to lead so many people out of darkness and into light that Satan has no more control over them. The apostle Paul never ran devils out of cities; he preached the Word that brought people out of darkness into light.

Satan has been the god of this world since Adam transferred the lease to him, and he will be here legally until his lease runs out—which is getting closer all the time!

Second, we humans live here legally. Anyone who lives in a flesh, blood, and bone body has legal residence on Earth. When someone loses his natural body, he no longer stays here. For a Christian, to be absent from the body is to be present with the Lord (2 Corinthians 5:8).

So first, Satan and all his cohorts live here legally. Second, humans live here legally. That is one of the reasons Jesus was made flesh and dwelt among us. Because He lived in a flesh, blood, and bone body, He could live here legally. The devil lives here legally, and you and I live here legally. God desires to do some things here, too—but He has to do them legally.

Another way to look at it is this: If you live in an apartment and pay rent to the owner, you live in the apartment legally. Someone else owns the building, but you have a lease on it, and as long as you pay your bills, you have a legal right to live there. The owner has no right to come, kick the door open, and say, "I want to come in." Even though he owns the building, once you sign the lease agreement, he has to have your permission to come in and do anything there.

God works on a legal basis, and although He has the power to do anything He wants on this Earth, He will never do anything to violate His law and give Satan room for accusation.

A Legal Invitation

We as humans living here legally can do basically what we want. But when God wants to do something on the Earth, He must do it by invitation. That is what we do in prayer—give God a legal invitation.

When we ask for "rain" according to His Word, and He begins to pour out His Spirit and power in a particular part of the world, the devil asks, "What are You doing here?" God says, "I have an invitation!"

When God begins to move on a nation because the people have cried out for Him to move, the devil says, "This is my place!" God says, "Not anymore—I've been invited. I have a legal invitation!"

When God wants to heal a missionary in the middle of Africa, He wakes someone at 4 o'clock in the morning to pray. God reaches out and heals the missionary, and the devil says, "You can't do that." God says, "Oh yes, I can. I have an invitation."

When we pray, we give God a legal right to move on the Earth. Jesus told us in Matthew 16:19, "...whatsoever thou shalt bind on earth shall be bound in heaven: and whatsoever thou shalt loose on earth shall be loosed in heaven."

The *King James* translation may be unclear to some of us. I like a translation I found in *The Word: The Bible From 26 Translations*. Included in this reference is E. V. Rieu's translation of Matthew 16:19: "...Whatever you forbid on earth, Heaven shall forbid and whatever you allow on earth, Heaven shall allow."

In other words, whatever we forbid here, heaven goes to work to make sure it is forbidden. If we allow something, heaven has no choice but to allow it. Why? Because through Jesus Christ, God has delegated authority to us, and it is up to us to do something with it. Jesus defeated the devil, took the keys of death, hell, and the grave, turned to His disciples, and said, "...All power [or all authority] is given unto me in heaven and in earth. Go ye therefore..." (Matthew 28:18,19). Jesus took the authority He had been given and transferred it to us!

We could explain it this way. If I gave you my pocket knife, the knife would be yours. If I wanted to do something with that knife, I couldn't—I no longer have the knife. You would have to be the one to do it, because I gave the knife to you. Jesus gave us His authority. He doesn't need the authority in heaven. The ones who need the authority are those who live on Earth, where the devil lives. If someone is going to use that delegated authority and either forbid or permit something to happen, who is it going to be? *You,* the one with the knife!

We see the same use of authority with a police officer. The government gives a police officer a uniform and a badge and sends him out to direct traffic. The officer may not be as large as the cars he is supposed to stop, but because we recognize the authority behind his position, we obey his commands.

If the officer says, "Stop," we stop; if he says, "Go," we go. Whatever decision the officer makes, the government backs him up. If we disobey the commands of the officer, we will have to answer to the government or the authority behind the officer.

It works the same way with God and the authority He delegated to us. Whatever we bind on Earth is bound in heaven, and whatever we loose on Earth is loosed in heaven. When we exercise our God-given authority, heaven will back us up!

"Why does God permit things to happen?" someone will ask.

Because *we* do! Whatever we permit, heaven will permit, and whatever we forbid, heaven will forbid.

Someone will say, "But I didn't know I had authority."

Suppose someone drives down the road at a high rate of speed. When the police officer pulls him over for speeding, he says, "But officer, I didn't see the sign. I didn't know there was a speed limit." Most likely the officer will not say, "Excuse me. Just go your way. You didn't know, so I'll let you go." No, the officer will probably say, "Ignorance of the law is no excuse."

We have the Law, the prophets, and the New Covenant; and whether we know it or not, it is up to us to exercise our God-given authority on the Earth. How do we exercise the authority that has been delegated to us? One way is through prayer. Prayer is doing business with God.

Every time we go to the Father in the Name of Jesus, we have just given God a legal invitation to come to this Earth and do what He wants to do. Whatever we forbid, heaven will forbid. Whatever we permit, heaven will permit. Whatever we ask, heaven is just waiting to back us up.

I am convinced that when the gifts of the Spirit begin to flow in a service and people are healed all over the congregation, it is because some saints have been on their faces before God. Someone has been asking God for the rain, asking for signs and wonders, and asking for the power of God to come in demonstration.

"God is limited by our prayer life. He can do nothing for mankind unless someone asks Him."

We don't want to limit God. Let's find out what God wants to do in the Earth and do some asking!

Chapter 3
Lifestyle of Prayer

There is so much to say on the subject of prayer, we could probably teach on it from now until Jesus comes and still not exhaust every aspect. Prayer is so important! The side of prayer we are probably most familiar with is the *asking* side, but prayer is not, "Gimme, gimme!" Although there is an asking side to prayer, it is not the only side.

There are all kinds of prayers. In fact, I heard someone say praise is the highest kind of prayer. We could come together, lift our hands toward heaven, praise God for an hour, and afterward say, "We had a great prayer meeting of the highest kind."

So there is not one set kind of prayer. Putting it simply, prayer is communion with God. We could say prayer is fellowship with God. Going beyond that, we could say prayer is carrying out God's will on Earth. In other words, prayer is doing business with God.

In this book, we are primarily concentrating on praying out the will and plan of God for our lives individually and for the Body of Christ at large. However, that is not to discount other types of prayer.

Ephesians 6:18 says, "Praying always with all prayer...." *The Amplified Bible* translates it, "Pray...with all [manner of] prayer...." Other types of prayer include the prayer of faith, prayer of consecration, prayer of agreement, and prayer of intercession, to name a few. They are all necessary.

When we speak of prayer that brings forth a move of God, a revival, an outpouring, or simply prayer for others, that is another side of prayer. But there is yet another side to prayer—the personal side.

Corporate prayer, which we will discuss later, is imperative in the day in which we live. However, its strength will be measured only by the personal prayer life of the individuals involved.

Prayer touches every area of our lives. It's like throwing a rock into a pond—the ripples go out and reach every shore. Developing our own prayer life is essential! The more we pray—particularly in the Holy Ghost or in other tongues (1 Corinthians 14:2)— the more sensitive we will become to the will and plan of God. God longs to bring His will to pass in the Earth and in us individually. He desires to have communion and fellowship and do business with us, His creation.

Developing our own prayer life makes prayer personal and causes things in our lives to be in order. Jesus said, "...pray, lest ye enter into temptation..." (Mark 14:38). A prayer life will help our spirit grow stronger than our flesh and help keep us out of the many temptations and problems we face in life. The more we "walk in the Spirit," the more we are able to "not fulfil the lust of the flesh" (Galatians 5:16).

James said by the Holy Ghost, "Is any among you afflicted?"—afflicted meaning "tempted, tested, tried or having a difficult time." James said if anyone is going through a hard time, "... Let *him* pray..." (James 5:13). A strong prayer life will help keep us out of afflictions and show us as how to deal with them and come out victoriously.

I remember knowing as a young boy that God had something for my life. When I was in the second grade, there was a teacher at my school who was a Christian. She and her husband pastored a Full Gospel church outside of town. I can vividly remember being out on the playground for recess one day, and this teacher walked right up to me, pointed her finger at me, and said, "Young man, God has something for you." I thought, *Yes, I know.* I had no idea what that meant, yet somehow inside I knew she was right. Children know things.

As a child I knew God had something for me, but as I got into my teenage years and yielded to peer pressure, that sensitivity I once had began to grow dim. I had no spiritual strength and wasn't going anywhere where my spirit could be fed. I never read a Bible. I never prayed. I didn't know I was supposed to do those things.

I loved God, yet I decided I wasn't interested in Him. I had my own plan for my life, and ministry was not part of it. So I ran for all I was worth to get away from God. I soon found, however, there is nowhere to run and nowhere to hide from God.

I thought I could get away by going to college, but I found God there, too—or I should say, God found me! I was born again my sophomore year at the state university I attended. There were people praying for me, and God had people planted everywhere to get my attention. It took just the right person to witness to me, and I accepted Jesus and got involved in a Christian college group.

When I went home for the summer, I received the baptism of the Holy Ghost in that same church pastored by the schoolteacher and her husband. They became my first real pastors. Then, when I returned to college, my group kicked me out for speaking in tongues! I didn't know what to do. I was trying to do my best to live for God, yet I didn't have anywhere to be fed spiritually. I was trying to be strong in myself, but the Bible says, "...be strong in the Lord..." (Ephesians 6:10).

How do we grow strong in the Lord? We know God's Word is the primary key, but our prayer life also has a lot to do with it. Jesus never said temptation wouldn't come; He said, "...pray, lest ye enter into temptation...." Prayer helps our spirit man be more developed than our flesh, and then our spirit can dominate us.

Jude 20 says, "But ye, beloved, building up yourselves on your most holy faith, *praying in the Holy Ghost*." "Yourself" is the real you—who you are on the inside—your spirit man. The Bible says you can build yourself up by praying in the Holy Ghost. It would amaze people how things that have kept them in bondage for years fall off them—simply by maintaining a consistent prayer life.

No More Graveclothes

We can draw a correlation from John 11, where Jesus raised Lazarus from the dead. This is a picture of our being born again and going from spiritual death to spiritual life. When Jesus came to the grave of his friend Lazarus, He said, "...Lazarus, come forth. And he that was dead came forth, *bound hand and foot with graveclothes*: and his face was bound about with a napkin..." (John 11:43,44). Lazarus bounded out of the grave alive, but there was one problem: He was still bound with graveclothes.

Sometimes people are born again (passing from spiritual death to spiritual life) but as they come into the family of God, their graveclothes follow them. Notice Jesus' response to Lazarus was not, "Throw him back in; he's not really alive." Jesus knew sometimes graveclothes will follow people until they have the opportunity to develop in the Word of God and grow spiritually. Jesus looked at His disciples and said, "...Loose him, and let him go."

When I was first born again, I "backslid" for the first three months. I didn't mean to, but I was still bound in those graveclothes. I did my best to live for God but just couldn't seem to do it. Finally, I decided the best thing for me to do was to move out of the college dorm. I moved back to my parents' home and drove the 60-minute commute to classes every day: 30 minutes there and 30 minutes back.

This was in the early '70s, and we didn't have all the cassette tapes and Christian radio stations we have today; consequently, the drive was rather boring.

I was baptized in the Holy Ghost, but I didn't know the purpose of praying in tongues. For some reason, one day I decided I was going to pray in tongues the whole way to school and the whole way back. The first thing I found was that praying in tongues sure made the time go faster! So five days a week I prayed in tongues an hour a day.

Do you know what I noticed? I was no longer trying to get rid of things. Instead, things were falling off me. The graveclothes were coming off! I didn't try to quit this habit or that habit; suddenly, I no longer had a desire for the things I used to do.

A prayer life will change us. That's why James said, "Is any among you afflicted? *let him pray....*" "Afflicted" does not mean sick. James gave instructions in James 5:14 to those who are sick. "Afflicted" means "to be suffering tests, trials, or tribulations." James didn't say, "Is any among you afflicted, let him go to eight hours of counseling." (Thank God for counseling if it's according to the Bible.) James didn't say, "Is any among you afflicted, let him call the prayerline and have someone else do his praying for him." No, James said for *you* to pray yourself.

Praying the Word

Sometimes people say, "I have a hard time praying. I pray a few minutes, and then I'm done." In developing a prayer life, sometimes it's good to go back through the New Testament, particularly to Paul's prayers. They can be found in Ephesians 1:15, Ephesians 3:14, and Colossians 1:9.

EPHESIANS 1:15-23
15 Wherefore I also, after I heard of your faith in the Lord Jesus, and love unto all the saints,
16 Cease not to give thanks for you, making mention of you in my prayers;
17 That the God of our Lord Jesus Christ, the Father of glory, may give unto you the spirit of wisdom and revelation in the knowledge of him:
18 The eyes of your understanding being enlightened; that ye may know what is the hope of his calling, and what the riches of the glory of his inheritance in the saints,
19 And what is the exceeding greatness of his power to us-ward who believe, according to the working of his mighty power,
20 Which he wrought in Christ, when he raised him from the dead, and set him at his own right hand in the heavenly places,
21 Far above all principality, and power, and might, and dominion, and every name that is named, not only in this world, but also in that which is to come:
22 And hath put all things under his feet, and gave him to be the head over all things to the church,
23 Which is his body, the fulness of him that filleth all in all.

EPHESIANS 3:14-21
14 For this cause I bow my knees unto the Father of our Lord Jesus Christ,
15 Of whom the whole family in heaven and earth is named,

16 That he would grant you, according to the riches of his glory, to be strengthened with might by his Spirit in the inner man;
17 That Christ may dwell in your hearts by faith; that ye, being rooted and grounded in love,
18 May be able to comprehend with all saints what is the breadth, and length, and depth, and height;
19 And to know the love of Christ, which passeth knowledge, that ye might be filled with all the fulness of God.
20 Now unto him that is able to do exceeding abundantly above all that we ask or think, according to the power that worketh in us,
21 Unto him be glory in the church by Christ Jesus throughout all ages, world without end. Amen.

COLOSSIANS 1:9-14
9 For this cause we also, since the day we heard it, do not cease to pray for you, and to desire that ye might be filled with the knowledge of his will in all wisdom and spiritual understanding;
10 That ye might walk worthy of the Lord unto all pleasing, being fruitful in every good work, and increasing in the knowledge of God;
11 Strengthened with all might, according to his glorious power, unto all patience and longsuffering with joyfulness;
12 Giving thanks unto the Father, which hath made us meet to be partakers of the inheritance of the saints in light:
13 Who hath delivered us from the power of darkness, and hath translated us into the kingdom of his dear Son:
14 In whom we have redemption through his blood, even the forgiveness of sins.

In times of prayer, we can go to these Holy Ghost-inspired Scriptures, which are really prayers Paul prayed, and pray them over ourselves. We can pray them over our families, over our pastor, and over our staff. I have found praying them to be a successful means of praying for myself and others. Why? The Holy Ghost gave these prayers to the apostle Paul, and what worked in Paul's day will work today, because spiritual things never grow old.

I have heard people say, "I just don't have that much to pray about."

I can challenge you on that! If you find everything there is to pray about and start praying, I guarantee you will not be finished by tomorrow night. Is there something you haven't fully understood in the area of divine healing? Are you having trouble seeing something in the area of prosperity? Go to Ephesians 1:18, and begin to pray: "The eyes of your understanding being enlightened...." *The Amplified Bible* says, "...the eyes of your heart flooded with light...." Insert your name there: "That the God of our Lord Jesus Christ, the Father of glory, may give unto *me* the spirit of wisdom and revelation in the knowledge of him: The eyes of *my* understanding being enlightened...."

Someone may ask, "Isn't that selfish?"

No. Sometimes we have to get things right ourselves before we can help anyone else.

God gave us a prayer to help our inner man become flooded with light. How does it work? "The entrance of thy words giveth light..." (Psalm 119:130). The prayers God gave Paul will help us have revelation knowledge of God's Word. Revelation of God's Word produces heart knowledge, not just head knowledge.

Someone will say, "I prayed that prayer once."

Did it work? Are you satisfied? Notice Paul said in Ephesians 1:16, "*Cease not* to give thanks for you, making mention of you in my prayers." There are some prayers— the prayer of faith for example—that we pray only once for that specific need. Smith Wigglesworth said, "If you ask God seven times for the same thing, six times are in unbelief."*

It is the same in the area of healing. The first time we pray, we believe we receive. The next time we pray for the same thing, we have just negated the first prayer. We don't need to keep asking for the things that legally belong to us; we can just reach out with the hand of faith, grab hold of them, and continue to thank God for them.

There are other types of prayer, however, where we pray for things that have not been bought and paid for by the precious blood of the Lord Jesus. These are things that are not a part of the redemptive plan—such as the prayer of consecration—but they are things God wants in our lives.

We see an example of the prayer of consecration in Luke 22:42, when Jesus prayed, "...nevertheless not my will, but thine, be done." Things that are an increasing, life-long progression, such as our "spiritual eyes" being flooded with light, are things that should be prayed frequently. We would do ourselves a favor if we would follow Paul's example and pray the prayers he prayed over ourselves on a daily basis.

We also should take time to pray these prayers for others. After that, we can spend some time praying in other tongues. Before long, we'll have 60 minutes of praying in, and we still won't be finished.

When we start praying this way, we will never run out of things to pray for.

When we put these things into practice, we will begin to develop a prayer life of our own. If an hour is

---

*Stanley Howard Frodsham, *Smith Wigglesworth: Apostle of Faith* (Springfield, Missouri: Gospel Publishing House, 1948), page 122.

too long to pray, don't be under condemnation about it. If five minutes is all you can do, pray fervently for that five minutes, and soon you will stretch it to six.

"There is therefore now no condemnation to them which are in Christ Jesus..." (Romans 8:1). You cannot pattern your prayer life after someone else's. You have to find what works for you and stretch it from there. In time you'll be so thrilled with prayer you'd rather pray than do anything else.

Great Men and Women of Prayer

If you read history books about the great men and women of God through the past 2000 years, you can see that anyone who had a great ministry also had a corresponding prayer life. People can have a wonderful gift, and it will carry them for a while, but no gift will last apart from communion with God.

Jesus is our best example. Some may think Jesus didn't have to have a prayer life because, after all, He was the Word, is the Word, and always will be the Word. Jesus is the Son of God, but while He was on the Earth, He ministered as a man anointed by God. Anytime Jesus prepared to minister to the multitudes, heal the sick, cleanse the lepers, or raise the dead, He first went somewhere to pray. Notice He didn't take long naps to rest. Don't misunderstand me; we have to give our bodies a rest. Epaphroditus worked himself nigh unto death for the sake of the ministry according to Philippians 2:30. But one thing I have noticed personally is that I don't grow weary *physically* unless I push too long and hard and become drained *spiritually*.

Jesus had multitudes pulling on Him, touching Him, and drawing on His anointing. The way He refreshed Himself after these times was to go to the mountains to pray. He would go up into the mountains and pray all night, then come back down and minister to the multitudes. Then He'd go back up again to commune with God and get refreshed.

Notice what Luke 11:1 says: "And it came to pass, that, as he was *praying* in a certain place...." Prayer was a major part of Jesus' earthly life. Jesus' prayer life was so effective and left such an impression on His disciples, they asked in that same verse, "...Lord, teach us to pray, as John also taught his disciples." The disciples watched Jesus pray and recognized He had something they didn't, and they wanted it. Jesus had fellowship and communion with the Father. If Jesus needed that, so do we!

Isn't it interesting the disciples never asked Jesus, "Teach us to prophesy," or "Teach us to raise the dead."

What was it about Jesus' prayer life that made the disciples want Him to teach them to pray? Fruit. Apparently they watched Jesus pray things out; then they watched Him walk things out. They watched Him pray out healings, then walk out healings. They saw Him pray out miracles, then walk out miracles. They witnessed Him asking God to do things. Then He went out and God did them. Jesus had His prayers answered— His prayers had fruit!

I reasoned if the disciples saw the fruit of Jesus' prayer life and asked Him to teach them to pray, I could learn some things myself by studying Jesus' prayer life.

One thing I found is that Jesus' prayer life had a direct effect on the anointing upon His life. We looked at this verse from another angle earlier. Notice Luke 3 and how Jesus' prayer life affected other areas of His life.

LUKE 3:21,22
21 Now when all the people were baptized, it came to pass, that Jesus also being baptized, AND PRAYING, THE HEAVEN WAS OPENED,

22 And THE HOLY GHOST DESCENDED in a bodily shape like a dove upon him, and a voice came from heaven, which said, Thou art my beloved Son; in thee I am well pleased.

Jesus went to the Jordan River to be baptized by John the Baptist. John's baptism was a baptism of repentance, but Jesus had nothing to repent of—He was our sinless, spotless sacrifice. Jesus was baptized to fulfill Scripture. He obeyed God even when it didn't make any sense to the natural mind.

His obedience also had a direct effect on the anointing on His life. It was when Jesus was baptized in water that the Spirit of God descended upon Him. At that point, Jesus received the Spirit without measure. The anointing of God came on Him and remained on Him for the duration of His ministry (John 2:11; Luke 4:18,19).

Notice in particular Luke 3:21 in the *New King James Version*: "...Jesus also was baptized; and while He prayed, the heaven was opened." Praying will open heaven! Jesus was obedient to go to the river to be baptized, and when He came out of the water He was praying or communing with God. Heaven opened, and the anointing of God came down upon Him. If the Church will learn to pray, we will get heaven opened in these last days, the anointing will come down, the rain will fall, and the world will change!

What about the apostle Paul's prayer life? We know what his prayer life was like by his writings. Paul wrote all of the prayers mentioned earlier, and then said in First Corinthians 14:18, "I thank my God, I speak with tongues more than ye all."

Other than the Lord Jesus Himself, Paul is the only one we have record of who said, "I finished my course." Paul wrote more than half of the New Testament and planted churches across two continents. He's the kind of man I want to follow. The prayers Paul recorded are as effective today as the day he wrote them.

Another man I have read after is the great missionary John G. Lake. He was a man mightily used of God and had tremendous healings and miracles in his ministry. He said the effectiveness of what God called him to do and the fruit of it was directly related to his prayer life. Dr. Lake also said if there was any area he could be considered excessive in, it was praying in other tongues. When I read that, I thought, *If this is what praying in tongues can produce, I am going to push out to the edge of it. If it worked for John G. Lake, it can work for me.*

Whether it be ministry, business, or another area of life, if we follow the example of any man or woman God has used, we can achieve the same success they did. The more successful we want to be, the more successful prayer life it will require, because prayer touches every area of our lives.

People say, "Prayer is just for the preacher." No, prayer is for the Church.

Every area of life is directly related to our prayer life. If preachers need prayer to be successful in preaching, businessmen need prayer to be successful in business. And a strong prayer life will help us have a successful family.

One minister wrote, "The further I go in ministry, the more I have to do during the day. The more I have to do during the day, the earlier I have to wake up to pray to get ready to do all there is to do." Most of us think the more we have to do, the more it is going to cut into our prayer time. This man, however, planned his entire day around prayer. If he had more to do, he woke up an hour earlier to be able to pray more to prepare for the day.

Pray Without Ceasing

We can look to godly men and women as examples in prayer, but the bottom line is that we have to find what works best for us. Having a lifestyle of prayer is so essential. In First Thessalonians 5, Paul gave us three important things to do constantly to help us maintain a lifestyle of prayer.

> 1 THESSALONIANS 5:16-18
> 16 REJOICE evermore.
> 17 PRAY without ceasing.
> 18 In every thing GIVE THANKS: for this is the will of God in Christ Jesus concerning you.

Paul said by the Holy Ghost that if we are constantly rejoicing, constantly praying, and constantly giving thanks, we will find ourselves in the will of God.

We attended a meeting in another country where a young man seated on the front row prayed constantly during the entire service. It was a little distracting, because we could hear him praying in other tongues under his breath the whole time. I finally asked the pastor about this young man.

"Oh," the pastor said, "he saw that verse 'Pray without ceasing,' and he thinks he is out of the will of God if he ever stops praying."

"My goodness," I said, "that would wear a person out! Has anyone ever told him when he chews and swallows he's not praying? Doesn't he know he is out of the will of God when he eats? What about when he goes to bed at night? Has anyone ever told him he has stepped out of the will of God when he falls asleep?

"Yes. We tried to tell him, but he hasn't gotten it yet."

I said, "Well, he will."

What Paul meant by "Pray without ceasing" is simply stay in fellowship with God. Always stay in an attitude of prayer. That does not mean we pray in tongues 24 hours a day. We have to find what works best for us individually.

An hour of prayer may seem like a long time to some people. Maybe it's better for them to start with five minutes. Eventually five minutes won't be long enough to cover everything, and it will take 10 minutes of prayer. When that doesn't seem long enough, it may take 15 or 20 minutes to pray things through. Sometimes we have to "stretch" our prayer life. The more we pray, the more we will grow conscious of spiritual things instead of natural things, and prayer will become easier and more enjoyable.

It is important for us to understand that we cannot pattern our prayer life after someone else's. For example, my schedule changes every day. The other day I woke up at 5 o'clock in the morning, headed to the airport, and flew nearly all day. I had gone to bed at 1 o'clock that morning, so it was not possible for me to spend an hour in my prayer closet that day.

If Janet and I are traveling overseas we spend extended periods of time on airplanes. Airplanes are not the easiest places to get into a "spirit of prayer." Consequently, having a regimented prayer schedule has not worked well for me. For some people, it does work well.

During meetings, my best time to pray seems to be in the afternoon. For some people, the best time to pray is in the early morning. Others do better at night. The bottom line is that we all have to find what works best for us and not get under condemnation about it.

Wigglesworth: A Man of Prayer

I like what Smith Wigglesworth said about prayer. He was a man greatly used by God in his ministry. Reportedly, 23 people were raised from the dead under his ministry. He touched nations all over the world with creative miracles, signs and wonders, healings, and demonstrations of the Spirit in his meetings.

Wigglesworth walked in such power, people were convicted of their need for Jesus just by being in his presence! The man really didn't start his ministry until he was in his fifties, and he didn't enter into the fullness of it until he was in his sixties. You may think a man like that would pray at least 12 hours a day.

Someone once asked Wigglesworth, "What is your prayer life like? How much do you pray?" I found his answer interesting. He said, "I don't spend more than half an hour in prayer at one time." That would shock some people if they didn't know the rest of what he said. "I don't spend more than half an hour in prayer at one time, but I never go more than a half hour without praying."

Wigglesworth developed a lifestyle of walking with God. Prayer was not just one part of his day; it was a *vital* part of his daily life. He communed and fellowshipped with God all the time. That is what worked for him. And we need to find what works for us.

We need to develop a prayer life of our own. If we have a life of rejoicing, giving thanks, and praying, we will walk in the will of God. In fact, if this is our lifestyle, we will have trouble *not* finding the will of God for our lives!

Chapter 4
Praying In the Spirit

In John 16, Jesus gave His disciples instructions concerning the Holy Ghost. He said in verse 7, "Nevertheless I tell you the truth; It is expedient for you that I go away...."

Can you imagine Jesus saying that to His disciples? The world had waited thousands of years for the Messiah to come, and finally He arrived. He spent 33 years on Earth—the last few with His disciples, who watched Him heal the sick, cleanse the lepers, raise the dead, cast out devils, and supernaturally meet their personal needs.

Suddenly Jesus told them He was leaving! This must have been difficult for them to understand. Not only did Jesus say He was leaving; He also said it would be *better* for the disciples for Him to go. How could it be better?

Jesus explained in verse 7, "...for if I go not away, the Comforter will not come unto you; but if I depart, I will send him unto you." In other words, Jesus said He would send someone else in His place. Notice He didn't say *a comforter*, He said *another comforter*. Jesus seemed to put the Holy Ghost on the same level of importance as Himself. He said, "If I go, it will be better or more profitable for you, because *another comforter* will come."

How could that be better? When Jesus was on the Earth, He could only be in one place at one time. When He was with the Father in the beginning, He was omniscient, omnipresent, and omnipotent. But when He was made flesh and dwelt on Earth, He stripped

Himself of that power. He was no longer all-knowing and all-powerful, and He could no longer be everywhere at one time. So when the Comforter came, everything Jesus did for us on an individual basis, the Holy Ghost could do for the whole world at the same time.

Heaven's Conductor

In essence, everything Jesus bought and paid for with His own precious blood would have been useless if the Father did not have a way to deliver those blessings to us. We needed a conductor to bring heaven's blessings to Earth. If there was a power plant producing electricity outside of town, but there was no means to bring that power to our home, we would be sitting in the dark. The world was in darkness and would have remained in darkness, even though Jesus went to the cross, fulfilled the plan of redemption, and sat down at the Father's right hand. It took the work of the Holy Spirit—heaven's Conductor—to deliver what Jesus bought and paid for to Earth.

Heaven has all we need! In fact, everything heaven has belongs to us, but it takes a certain "atmosphere" for those things to manifest for us on Earth. What is that atmosphere? The Holy Ghost. He brings the blessings of God and converts them into what mankind needs.

Jesus said the Holy Ghost would have some specific jobs to do on Earth. In John 16:13 He said, "Howbeit when he, the Spirit of truth, is come, he will guide you into all truth: for he shall not speak of himself; but whatsoever he shall hear, that shall he speak: and he will shew you things to come."

Thank God, we have a Guide! The world lies in darkness, but we have the Spirit of Truth to light our pathway and show us things to come. Jesus went on to say in the next verses:

JOHN 16:14,15
14 He shall glorify me: for HE SHALL RECEIVE OF MINE, AND SHALL SHEW IT UNTO YOU.
15 All things that the Father hath are mine: therefore said I, that HE SHALL TAKE OF MINE, AND SHALL SHEW IT UNTO YOU.

Did you know it glorifies Jesus when the Holy Ghost takes what belongs to Jesus and shows it to us? What belongs to Jesus? He told us in verse 15, *"All things* that the Father hath are mine...."* Anything that belongs to the Father also belongs to the Son, and the Bible says the Holy Ghost will take those things and show them to us.

The word "show" is not easily understood in the *King James* translation. In *The Amplified Bible*, that verse is translated, "He will honor and glorify Me, because He will take of (receive, draw upon) what is Mine and will reveal (declare, disclose, transmit) it to you." In other words, the Holy Ghost will take what belongs to the Father and reveal, declare, disclose, and transmit it to us.

Declare, Disclose, and Transmit

When I saw this in the Scriptures, I thought, *How does He declare, disclose, and transmit these things?* I know the first way is through the Word of God. The second way is by the witness of the Spirit or the leading of the Holy Ghost. But there is a third way found in John 16.

JOHN 16:20-24
20 Verily, verily, I say unto you, That ye shall weep and lament, but the world shall rejoice: and ye

**shall be sorrowful, but your sorrow shall be
turned into joy.**

**21 A woman when she is in travail hath sorrow,
because her hour is come: but as soon as she is
delivered of the child, she remembereth no more
the anguish, for joy that a man is born into the
world.**

**22 And ye now therefore have sorrow: but I will
see you again, and your heart shall rejoice, and
your joy no man taketh from you.**

**23 AND IN THAT DAY, YE SHALL ASK ME
NOTHING. Verily, verily, I say unto you,
WHATSOEVER YE SHALL ASK THE FATHER IN
MY NAME, HE WILL GIVE IT YOU.**

**24 Hitherto have ye asked nothing in my name:
ask, and ye shall receive, that your joy may be full.**

What day was Jesus talking about? He was referring
to the day when He would no longer be on Earth—the
day of the New Covenant or day of grace in which we
live. Until this time, the disciples had looked to Jesus to
meet their needs. He answered their questions, helped
them pay their bills, and fed them. Now He was telling
the disciples things were going to change.

He said, "...In that day ye shall ask me nothing.
Verily, verily, I say unto you, *Whatsoever ye shall ask
the Father in my name*, he will give it you" (verse 23).
The disciples could now go to the Father directly for
themselves because of what Jesus did.

Jesus said in verse 24, "Hitherto," or up until this
point, "have ye asked nothing in my name: ask, and ye
shall receive, that your joy may be full." The Father is
the One who meets our needs, and He works through
the Son. That is why James wrote James 1:16,17, "Do
not err, my beloved brethren. Every good gift and every
perfect gift is from above, and cometh down from the
Father of lights, with whom is no variableness, neither
shadow of turning."

Access Through the Name

Because we live under the New Covenant, we no longer go to Jesus to meet our needs. We go to the Father in Jesus' Name. Prayer is directed to the Father. Jesus provided a way for us to have access to the Father ourselves—He shed His blood and gave us His Name.

> **JOHN 16:26,27**
> **26 At that day ye shall ASK IN MY NAME: and I say not unto you, that I will pray the Father for you:**
> **27 FOR THE FATHER HIMSELF LOVETH YOU,** because ye have loved me, and have believed that I came out from God.

Thank God Jesus has provided a new and living way to access the Father! Prayer is the third way the Holy Ghost will reveal what the Father has for us. The Holy Ghost will declare, disclose, and transmit what belongs to us through prayer.

Our Helper in Prayer

Speaking of the Holy Ghost, Jesus said in John 14:16, "And I will pray the Father, and he shall give you another Comforter, that he may abide with you for ever." Another word for Comforter is the word *paraclete*, which means "one called alongside to help."

The Amplified Bible gives seven different meanings for the word *paraclete*: Comforter, Counselor, Helper, Intercessor, Advocate, Strengthener, and Standby. That is one reason God wants us to be full of the Holy Ghost. The more we are filled with Him, the more He is able to do these jobs in our lives.

Has anyone ever needed a helper? Then get full of the Helper.

Does anyone need counsel? The Church puts great emphasis on counseling, and the best way to receive counsel is to get full of the Counselor.

How about strength? Get full of the Strengthener.

Could anyone use some standby help? There is nothing like an extra boost from the Standby when we hit a tough place.

The Holy Ghost is all those things to us. But someone once said to me, *"The greatest help the Holy Ghost is to the Church is our Helper in prayer."*

The Holy Ghost knows everything. Jesus said the Holy Ghost will declare, disclose, and transmit what heaven has to us! The best way to receive from heaven is to get into heaven. We could say the best place to hear from the Spirit of God is to get *in the Spirit.* In fact, Paul said in Ephesians 6:18, "Praying always with all prayer and supplication *in the Spirit....*" One translation says, "Praying with all manner of prayer" or *all kinds* of prayer.

Praying With the Spirit
and the Understanding

Notice Paul did not say, "Praying always with all kinds of prayer *and* praying in the Spirit." He wasn't referring to two different kinds of prayer. No, Paul said, "Praying always with all kinds of prayer and supplication in the Spirit." There are all kinds of prayer: the prayer of faith, the prayer of agreement, the prayer of binding and loosing, and the prayer of intercession, for example. What often happens is, we try to pray all these different kinds of prayers, and then we switch over and start praying in other tongues.

What Paul suggests, however, is for us to pray until we get in the Spirit, and then the Holy Ghost will take us into different kinds of prayer. When we pray that way, we will find our prayer life is more effective. The prayer of faith will be more effective if we pray it in the Spirit rather than from our head or mental realm. Praying in the Holy Ghost, praying in other tongues, for a while will get us out of the natural realm and over into God's territory, where our prayers are not just coming out of our head or understanding.

Don't misunderstand me—there is a place for praying with our understanding. Praying with our understanding is when we look in the Scriptures, find out what God said, and pray it back to Him. But when we pray in the Spirit, we are praying things we don't know anything about.

First Corinthians 14:2 says, "For he that speaketh in an unknown tongue speaketh not unto men, but unto God: for no man understandeth him; howbeit in the spirit he speaketh mysteries." When we pray in other tongues, we are speaking to God. Praying in other tongues gets us in the Spirit, where we may not know what we are praying for; in fact, we are speaking *mysteries*.

That is our infirmity—not knowing what to pray for as we ought. Romans 8:26 says, "Likewise the Spirit also helpeth our infirmities: for we know not what we should pray for as we ought: but the Spirit itself maketh intercession for us with groanings which cannot be uttered." Notice that verse does not say, "...for we don't know *how* to pray as we ought...." It says, "...for we know not *what* we should pray for as we ought...." We have an unction or a stirring to pray, and we don't know what to do.

Thank God for the Holy Ghost! We start praying in the Spirit by the unction of the Holy Ghost and start speaking mysteries to God. We can use both kinds of prayer: Praying with our understanding—praying what the Bible says—and praying in the Holy Ghost, where we touch things we don't know anything about.

Prayer affects every area of our lives. The prophet Isaiah made reference to prayer in Isaiah 28.

> **ISAIAH 28:9-11**
> **9 Whom shall he teach knowledge? and whom shall he make to understand doctrine? them that are weaned from the milk, and drawn from the breasts.**
> **10 For precept must be upon precept, precept upon precept; line upon line, line upon line; here a little, and there a little:**
> **11 For with stammering lips and another tongue will he speak to this people.**

Paul quotes these Scriptures in First Corinthians 14:21,22: "In the law it is written, With men of other tongues and other lips will I speak unto this people; and yet for all that will they not hear me, saith the Lord. Wherefore tongues are for a sign, not to them that believe, but to them that believe not: but prophesying serveth not for them that believe not, but for them which believe."

We can see that Isaiah was speaking about the blessing to come in New Testament times—speaking with other tongues. He also foretold of some of the benefits related to this kind or prayer.

First, Isaiah asked, "Whom shall he teach knowledge? And whom shall he make to understand?..." He went on to say, "For with stammering lips and another tongue will he speak...." Isaiah was referring to the future experience of praying in other tongues. There is something about praying—particularly in the Holy Ghost or with other tongues—that will cause us to have clearer understanding or revelation of the Word of God.

I have received much more revelation from praying than I have from simply studying. That does not mean we should set studying aside; but if we study and then pray in the Holy Ghost, it will help what we've studied to turn from simply head knowledge to heart revelation. Why? Because praying in the Holy Ghost takes us out of the natural realm and into the supernatural realm—out of the flesh and into the realm of the Spirit.

Sometimes praying in the Spirit is just a matter of quieting the mind so we can get *in the Spirit*. When we get over in the Spirit, prayer becomes a lot more fun. What does it mean to pray "in the Spirit"? It simply means we become more conscious of prayer than we do of anything else. We pray more from our hearts than our heads. That does not mean we become unconscious or end up in a cloud somewhere. It means we pray to the point where our minds finally give up and become quiet. And the spirit man rises up and dominates in prayer.

I think most believers have set themselves to pray for a certain period of time—an hour, for example. We start by praying in our understanding, and then we pray in other tongues. We think, *I must have prayed for at least an hour and a half.* Then we look at our watch, and it has been four minutes and 35 seconds.

So we start praying in other tongues again and say, "Surely it has been at least an hour." We check our watch again, and this time it has been a whole eight minutes! Has anyone ever been there? There may be other times we go to pray and say, "I must have been praying about 20 minutes." When we check our watch, it has been an hour and 15 minutes! What is the difference? One is where we have gotten more "in the Spirit" and one is where we have not.

Road Map in Prayer

Someone may say, "But I have never been to that place in prayer."

That's all right. Just stay with it. Don't give up.

Throughout the year, we minister at different churches across the country. Usually we fly to our destination. When we arrive in the city, we rent a car and drive to our hotel and then drive from our hotel to the church.

The first time we visit a particular church, we have to have a map and good directions to follow. Usually someone from the church has written them down for us, and we follow them carefully. The next night, we may have to refresh ourselves with the directions, but by the third night we no longer need to use a map. We may need to concentrate a little to make the right turns, but the route is already familiar to us. We don't even have to think about how to get there—it is almost unconscious.

It is the same way with getting in the Spirit in prayer. Sometimes it seems we have to pray and pray and pray just to get to the place where our minds are quiet. Then the next time it is like, "I have been here before. I may not have the exact directions, and I am going to have to work on this, but this is familiar territory."

After enough times, we won't even have to think about it anymore. We will know where to go and how to get there. That is when we can be more in the Spirit than in the flesh in prayer, and prayer will become a pleasure. Once we find the way, it gets easier every time.

Praying in other tongues—praying in the Holy Ghost, getting in the Spirit—takes a while, but stay with it, because that is where we will find the mysteries God has hidden for us.

What is the greatest mystery in life? The future. And prayer is one of the major keys that allows us access into the will and plan of God for our lives.

Chapter 5
Praying Out the Future

In looking through the Scriptures, we find God is an investor. He is always planning for the future. In Revelation 13:8, He called Jesus "...the Lamb slain from the foundation of the world." God doesn't live from day to day; He invests for the future. We are to be imitators of God (Ephesians 5:1), so we ought to be doing the same thing.

Ecclesiastes 11:1 shows us how Israel invested for their future: "Cast thy bread upon the water: for thou shalt find it after many days." The children of Israel took their seed, ate part, kept some for their journey, and then threw the rest on the waters, planting for their future. The water carried the seed downstream and left it on the banks of the river where all the rich soil was deposited. By the time the Israelites arrived there, they had a harvest waiting for them!

People say, "Oh, it costs so much to serve God."

No, serving God is *an investment!* Every time we obey God in giving finances, in prayer, or walking by faith, we are investing into His kingdom and our future. God dealt with me years ago on planting faith for the future. In Luke 17, Jesus said to His disciples:

LUKE 17:3,4
3 Take heed to yourselves: If thy brother trespass against thee, rebuke him; and if he repent, forgive him.
4 And if he trespass against thee seven times in a day, and seven times in a day turn again to thee, saying, I repent; thou shalt forgive him.

If someone does something to agitate you, and you say, "Don't do that; it really bothers me," and they repent and apologize, that is one thing. But if it happens every hour on the hour, it will grow old in a hurry.

Jesus said there should be no end to our forgiving. The disciples' response to this command was, "Lord, Increase our faith" (Luke 17:5). They wanted *Jesus* to do something with their faith. But Jesus put the responsibility right back on their shoulders and said in verse 6, "...If ye had faith as a grain of mustard seed, ye might say unto this sycamine tree, Be thou plucked up by the root, and be thou planted in the sea; and it should obey you."

I always thought Jesus meant, "If you had faith the *size* of a grain of mustard seed." A mustard seed is the smallest seed, but when planted becomes the greatest among herbs. What Jesus said, however, was, "...If ye had faith *as* a grain of mustard seed...." What do you do with a seed? You plant it. Your faith may not be much as a seed, but when you plant that faith, it will grow.

What causes faith to grow? The first thing that gives our faith the capacity for growth is planting faith where it can grow. The second thing that causes our faith to grow is feeding on the Word of God. I saw this in the Scriptures and thought, *If I want my faith to work for me in a situation 10 years down the road, I had better plant that seed now and give it time to grow.*

Faith is like a seed, and when I understood that, I began to plant faith seed all over the world. I planted my faith for open doors to minister in Europe. I planted my faith for building facilities, transportation, and finances. I put this into practice in 1979, and I am still reaping benefits from it to this day.

Planting Prayer for the Future

I thought, *If I can plant faith for my future, I can plant prayer for my future, too.* A number of years ago, the Holy Ghost spoke to my heart and said, "You are a half step behind." I knew immediately He meant I was a half step behind in prayer. We had come to the place where we were out ahead of our prayers. So, we called some friends together for extended times of prayer until we caught up.

Another time, the Holy Ghost spoke to me and said, "You're a step behind." So again, we caught up in prayer. Then one day it dawned on me: If we could be *behind* in prayer, we could just as easily be *ahead* in prayer. Why not plant our prayers and get them working ahead of us? We can pray about our future, pray about God's plan for our lives, and pray things through long before we get there.

In the Book of Deuteronomy, God showed Israel where to go, where to pitch their tents, and even drove out their enemies before them. Deuteronomy 1:33 says, "Who went in the way before you, to search you out a place to pitch your tents in, in fire by night, to shew you by what way ye should go, and in a cloud by day." God was always the God who went before them—and God has never changed.

I grew tired of getting to certain places or situations and feeling like I was running into a brick wall. So instead of falling on my face and crying out, "God, what am I going to do?" I decided I was going to double up on prayer concerning my future, plant my prayers, and allow God to start working on my future before I even got there.

God is the God who goes before us if we keep our prayer life active and rely on the Holy Ghost to help us pray things through. We can pray things out months, weeks, and even years ahead of time. Then, when we arrive at the situation, instead of panicking, we have faith that God is already working on our behalf. If we run into "brick walls," we can back up and look for a hole to go through, knowing that through prayer, God has already gone ahead of us to work on the situation. So instead of living from disaster and miracle to disaster and miracle, we simply walk with God in the miraculous.

Praying Out the Plan

This is exactly what we did when it was time to start our first DOMATA Bible school in Europe. Janet and I had never set up a school before. We didn't know the first thing about setting up a school. In fact, I remember telling God, "You have the wrong people, Lord. We have never done this before."

The interesting thing was, about the time God began to deal with us about the school, He was also dealing with the couple who were to oversee the school. God will never give us something to do that we can do ourselves. Faith pleases God, so in order to set up the school, we were going to have to trust Him in every step.

We knew we had heard from God, so I said, "Lord, we don't even know where to put a school, so You are going to have to show us." Suddenly it dropped on the inside of us that the first school needed to be in Tallinn, Estonia. However, we didn't instantly jump into a major move. We had been praying fervently and consistently for nearly two years concerning these schools.

We took the next logical step and traveled to Tallinn. "Now what do we do, Lord?" we asked. We couldn't very well jump in a taxi and say, "Take us to the nearest place that would work well for a school."

Estonia is a country of approximately 1.5 million people, the majority of whom live in Tallinn. There are countless buildings and few English-speaking people. Therefore, it is not the easiest place to start investigating potential school facilities.

There we were, standing in the middle of the main square in Tallinn, asking God what to do. He is the God who goes before us, and we knew we had already prayed this through. We knew we had planted prayer for our future. Janet and I and another couple went to our hotel room and began to pray. We spent hours praying, and then we hit the streets of Tallinn.

"What were we praying about?" We knew we already had this prayed through, but we wanted our spirits sensitive. Praying in the Holy Ghost makes us more sensitive to the will and leading of God.

After we prayed, the four of us began to walk until we felt "pulled" to a building where we knew a church met. It was really too large a facility for what we needed. Inside the building, we noticed one stairway going up to where the church met, but then we noticed a dingy old stairway leading down to what almost looked like a dungeon.

We decided to explore, and we followed the stairway down to a huge wooden door. Behind the door we found a gorgeous room with stained-glass windows, beautiful paneling, and a fireplace. It was large enough to seat about 50 people. We talked to the manager of the building and found it was for rent. It was the perfect facility for us to use the first year school was in session.

Everywhere we have gone to open a school, God has supernaturally gone ahead and provided the location and the facilities we needed. And we know there is more to come. Why? Because we have prayed things through ahead of time. We have been asking God in advance.

How does He do it? God is not in time—He is in eternity. That means He can go back a 1000 years or go ahead 100 years and start working things out for us.

Praying Out the Future

"But if you don't know the future, how do you know what to pray?"

One way in particular we can pray out our future is by praying in the Holy Ghost. As we noted earlier, praying in the Holy Ghost will make us sensitive to the will and plan of God.

Jeremiah 33:3 says, "Call unto me and I will answer thee, and shew thee great and mighty things, which thou knowest not." When we don't know what to do or where to go, we can call on God, and He said He would answer us and show us great and mighty things that we *know not.*

The margin of my Bible says, "Call unto me and I will answer thee, and shew thee great and *hidden things*...." Is there anything that is hidden from us? What about things concerning the future—where to go, what to do? God wants to show us things to come. How is He going to do that? One way is through prayer—times of calling on God.

The *New King James Version* translates Jeremiah 33:3, "Call to Me, and I will answer you, and show you great and *inaccessible things*...." There are people who need insight into the things of God: into the future, into His plan, into why things are or are not working as they should. The only way to access those things is through prayer.

God has given the Church a key to tapping into those inaccessible things. We find it in First Corinthians 14:2: "For he that speaketh in an unknown tongue speaketh not unto men, but unto God: for no man understandeth him; howbeit in the spirit he speaketh mysteries." In other words, when we speak in other tongues, we speak *mysteries* unto God. *The Amplified Bible* says it like this, "...He utters *secret truths* and *hidden things*." Remember Jeremiah 33:3? "Call unto me and I will answer thee, and shew thee great and *hidden things....*"

How do we start tapping into those hidden things? By praying in other tongues. When we pray in other tongues, we utter secret truths and hidden things. God is not hiding things *from* us; He is hiding them *for* us. He is not trying to hold things back; He is holding things in check.

It is almost like God is holding things in a bank vault until we get to the place where we need them. Then, through prayer, those hidden things are turned from *mysteries* to *revelation*. In the Old Testament, God told us what to do, (Jeremiah 33:3), and in the New Testament, He gave us the means to do it (1 Corinthians 14:2)!

Praying in the Holy Ghost gives us access into the mysteries in the future, into God's plan for our lives, and into things concerning our country, our church, our city, other nations, and even end times. God has given us a key to step into a realm or a secret place where we can do business with Him.

Probably the greatest need anyone has in the Body of Christ is to hear from heaven and know the plan of God. When we start praying in the Holy Ghost, we step into a place where it is so easy to hear from heaven. As we noted earlier, the best way to hear from the Holy Spirit is to get "in the Spirit." The most direction I have received in the last several years has been either in a time of prayer or right after a time of prayer.

Waiting on God

I attended a denominational church when I was first born again. Then I went off to college, and when I came home I visited the Full Gospel church I mentioned earlier. I spent some time there and noticed those folks had something different. Others stayed away from them and said, "That is of the devil." I never could understand how the devil was helping the Full Gospel bunch serve God better than the people who didn't have what they said the devil was giving!

I spent enough time at the church and saw enough fruit that I was baptized in the Holy Ghost. It was a small church, and almost every Sunday night we finished the service by going to the altar to wait on God.

Someone will say, "What do you mean, *wait* on God? Does that mean you sit and do nothing?" No, to wait on God means to be a waiter. It means you take your pad and pencil and say, "Sir, is there anything You would like? Is there anything You want me to do?" We basically waited on God and lifted our voices in prayer, mostly praying in the Holy Ghost. We did this week after week.

I remember one time I was praying in the Holy Ghost, and I said, "Lord, what do You want me to do?" I had been praying about college. At that time, I was taking pre-med courses as well as business administration courses. I didn't like anything I was doing. Nothing satisfied, and I didn't know what in the world I was going to do. All of a sudden, in this time of prayer, I saw in the Spirit a Scripture reference in front of me. The verse just flashed before me. At the time I didn't understand it, but within the past five or six years that verse has come to pass in my life. God told me way back there exactly what He called me to do!

Delight Yourself in the Lord

Later I attended Bible school and had the privilege of working in a helps capacity for another minister. Another young man and myself traveled all over the country on this minister's crusade team. It was a lot of hard work, but I wouldn't trade that time for anything in the world.

With two meetings a day, six days a week, and paperwork in between, it really cut into my prayer and study time. The other young man and I decided we had better make the best use of our time; so while I was driving I could pray, and he could study and pray, and after a few hours we would switch.

Once we were on our way from Tulsa, Oklahoma, to Houston, Texas, which is approximately a 10-hour drive. I had been driving for a while, so we decided to switch. I spent some time studying and reading my Bible. Then I closed my Bible and began to pray quietly in the Holy Ghost.

To give you some background, when I finished Bible school, I had told the Lord, "I will do anything You want me to do. I will go anywhere You want me to go. But if You give me a choice, there are two things I would rather not do. First, I would rather not work in a church. Second, I would rather not be a youth pastor."

Why I said that I don't know. I didn't have anything against those two things; it just seemed they did not line up with what was in my heart.

With that in mind, I was praying in the Holy Ghost and literally got *lost in prayer*. Suddenly I could "see" myself in a large room sitting on a chair. I had my Bible on my lap, and I was surrounded by young people. I realized I was in the fellowship hall of a church, and I was the youth pastor! I rebuked the thought and went back to reading my Bible.

It is in times of prayer that God will show us great and hidden things. When we start tapping into the One who knows past, present, and future, He will help us to pray things out before we even get there.

I studied some more, closed my Bible, and began to pray in the Holy Ghost again. Just like that, I was back in the same room, a Bible on my lap, surrounded by young people. I even knew the message I was teaching, and I knew I was the youth pastor. This happened all the way from Dallas to Houston.

We have to understand, God will not force us to do anything. But what He will do is put His desires in our heart. During a time of prayer on that trip to Houston, God dropped something inside of me.

The Bible says, "Delight thyself also in the Lord; and he shall give thee the desires of thine heart" (Psalm 37:4). That means, God will put His desires in us until His desires become our desires and our desires become His desires. I was delighting myself in the Lord. I was reading His Word and praying in the Holy Ghost.

By the time we arrived in Houston, I found myself saying, "God, give me a church where I can be a youth pastor!" What happened? Something changed on the inside. I prayed in the Holy Ghost, and I began to pray out the future.

It wasn't long after that we were at another meeting where I was working the book and tape table. I was standing there minding my own business when I noticed a gentleman walk by whom I had never seen before. I suddenly found myself clinging to the edge of the table, because when he walked by I started to lean over the table to grab his sleeve and say, "Sir, do you need a youth pastor?" I thought, *He is going to think I am nuts!*

It just so happened this man was a pastor, and he was at the meeting looking for a youth pastor. The minister I worked for told him, "I know just the man." To make a long story short, within 60 days I was serving as youth pastor at this man's church.

I had never been a youth pastor before. In fact, I had never even been in a youth group. I trained under the assistant pastor for a few weeks, and then he decided to turn the youth group over to me. The first night I went into the fellowship hall to hold a youth meeting, someone brought out a chair for me to sit on, just like the one I had seen in prayer. I sat on the chair, opened my Bible on my lap, and started teaching the message.

Suddenly I looked up and saw the young people sitting on the floor around me. I looked at my Bible and thought, *Dear Lord, this is exactly what I saw! It's the same room, the same chair, the same message, the same faces, and I am the youth pastor!*

God will show us things to come, and we can tap into those things through prayer. I just happened to *see* what was coming, but it doesn't always work that way. Sometimes things rise up on the inside along with a *knowing*.

God often deals with me ahead of time in this way; especially if it involves a major change. If there is something coming in the future, God starts dealing with me six months to two years in advance. This way I can pray things out ahead of time. I love the way God works!

Direction Comes in Prayer

I had been the youth pastor at this man's church for almost seven months when suddenly some things began to stir in my heart about change. I said, "Lord, I love it here. I don't want to leave." But God was dealing with me, so I began praying things out over the next few months.

During a Wednesday night prayer meeting at the church, I was praying in tongues when the Holy Ghost spoke to me and said, "It is time for you to go. Talk to the pastor, leave at this date (and He gave me a specific date). Then call this particular minister (He named the minister), and ask him if he has a position available for you. There will be a position for you, and you will serve there from May through October. In October, they will call you and ask you to be involved in another department. When they call, take the job; that is what you are supposed to do."

God told me all that in a time of prayer. I knew where the minister who the Holy Ghost had named was, so I stepped out during the meeting to call him. I explained to him that God had told me to leave my position as youth pastor and asked him if he had a position for me. He did, and it was exactly what the Holy Ghost had told me. In October, he called me into his office and told me he had something else for me to do in another department and asked if I would consider it. I said, "I work for you. If you want me to do it, I will." He did, I did, and it was the plan of God.

Direction always comes from praying in the Holy Ghost. "For he that speaketh in an unknown tongue speaketh not unto men, but unto God: for no man understandeth him; howbeit in the spirit he speaketh *mysteries*" (1 Corinthians 14:2). We can pray out the future. We can pray out God's plan for our lives. Then, instead of running into disasters and wondering what to do when we hit a brick wall, we can back up and start looking for the hole God has already knocked out for us to pass through to the other side.

Being Led by Prayer

For the first few years Janet and I were in ministry, we had our office in the den of our home. We started with a desk and a secretary. Then we had to hire another person to do the bookkeeping. Before long we had a second desk, a copy machine, filing cabinets, and a fax machine housed in our den. All we had left was a path from one end of the den to the other. The garage was taken over with books and tapes, and the closets were filling up fast.

About the same time we were running out of space, God began to deal with us about renting more office space. What does this have to do with prayer? A lot! I heard a well-known minister say, "Illustrations are like windows into a house." Illustrations help us see things more clearly.

Neither Janet nor I wanted to move into an office building, yet we felt we were supposed to. We began to pray along these lines. We knew the size of our den and decided we didn't need much more space than that—maybe a storefront somewhere that we could rent. We drove all over Tulsa looking for a facility that met our specifications.

We learned that sometimes the Holy Ghost works like a magnet, and He will either pull us to things or push us away from them. The more fine-tuned our spirits are, the more sensitive we will be to the leading of the Holy Spirit in our spirit. How do we develop our spirit? One way is through prayer.

Janet and I spent a lot of time praying and looking for the right building. Every time we drove past a particular area, something inside seemed to pull us to it. The area was an industrial park located fewer than two miles from our home. We pulled in and drove around it several times but thought, *This can't be it. There are no storefronts here.*

One week we pulled in to drive around and noticed not a storefront but a large building having nearly 10,000 square feet and surrounded by a parking lot. In front of the building was an old, beat-up For Sale sign. The building was vacant and looked like it had been for some time. We drove by laughing, "That is probably it!"

One evening we were at home praying together in the Holy Ghost when suddenly I found myself in the Spirit, praying some things in English. I prayed this not out of my head, but out of my heart.

I heard myself say, "Thank You dear Father for the facility You have for us. Thank You for the office space. We know You have been dealing with us to move into offices, and we know that is right. It is not our idea; it is Your idea. We know we have been looking at the wrong places, and we know You don't want us to rent a place. Thank you for letting us know You don't want us to rent, but to buy."

I was hearing myself say these things and I was thinking, *I do? He does? Are you sure?* I kept saying, "Father, I thank You for leading us by the Holy Ghost into a facility that is bigger than what we think we need. The one we want is way too small."

Suddenly my mind grabbed hold of what I was saying, and I stopped praying and said, "Amen." I looked at Janet, who was looking at me in surprise.

"Did you hear what you just prayed?" she asked.

I thought it was quite interesting, because I knew what I was praying was not coming out of my head but out of my spirit!

We started looking in the industrial area again, and this time these words came to me: "You're looking too small." I remembered the building we saw with the old For Sale sign. I have a background in real estate, so I had some people do research for me on the building. The building was repossessed and had been owned by the bank for more than a year.

When I contacted the bank, I already had a figure in my heart of what I wanted to pay for the building, but I backed my offer to a much lower amount. They laughed and threw it back at me. "That's fine," I said, "you need to sell it more than I need to buy it. If you are interested, give me a call."

We had a deadlock for a few months. We went back and forth for a while on the price. Then they called about six weeks later and said they were going to renovate the building and use it for rental space. I told them that sounded like a good idea, and they should do it.

Things were quiet for a while, then suddenly one day the bank called and wanted to know if I was still interested in the building. I said, "It depends on the price you want for it." They said they would take my last offer, which was the original figure I had in my heart!

Since then, the building has quadrupled in value. What used to be a two-lane street adjacent to us is now a five-lane street. A large retail store recently built a huge shopping center across the street from us. God knows how to turn a deal!

Everything we do prospers—but it all depends on being led by the Holy Ghost. Being led by the Holy Ghost is what happens in times of prayer.

Patterns in Prayer

I have learned it is a good idea to write down impressions that rise up out of our hearts in times of prayer. If it is direction we need for life—for next week, next month, or years down the road—it's a good idea to write down those impressions we get in prayer and keep track of them. Over a period of weeks or months, go back and see if there is a pattern that continues to surface. Sometimes through those things that keep rising up in our hearts, we will see what God is working out in our lives and future.

I have done this many times. I may write down a word or even whole phrases at times. At the time it may not make a bit of sense, but five or six months later when I look back, I find that God was having us pray out a whole plan. Thank God for the Holy Ghost! He was helping us pray out the plan way back there, and we didn't even know it. It is almost like He was bringing it out in code form so we couldn't mess it up.

We prayed out nearly every city in every nation where we currently have Bible schools. In fact, we usually knew the name of the city six months to a year before it was even time to start the school. The school located in France, for example, is currently headed by a couple with three young daughters. The girls had France in their hearts for a number of years before their family moved there. We also had France in our hearts, but we were waiting for the right time to set things in motion for a school.

One day I was praying in the Holy Ghost, and all of a sudden I heard myself say in English, "Versailles. Versailles. Versailles." I prayed a while longer, and again I heard myself say, "Versailles." I know Versailles is a French word as well as a city in France.

God told us to put the Bible schools in major cities because they are more easily accessible to airports where the visiting ministers can fly in and out. I was thinking about this and reasoned, *Versailles cannot be a place for a school, because it is located on the southern coast of France somewhere. I must be praying for someone to start a church in Versailles.* But as I continued to pray, I could not get away from the city of Versailles.

We have a prayer room in our ministry office with maps of the nations hanging on the walls. One day I decided to look at the European map while I was praying. I searched the map for Versailles, concentrating on the southern coast of France. I found Nice and Cannes, but no Versailles. I went back to my office, located an atlas, and looked up Versailles. I found Versailles is a suburb of Paris located 15 to 20 minutes from the Paris Orly Airport. Versailles is exactly where the school needed to be!

We can find out so much about our future through times of prayer. We can pray in the Holy Ghost and hear from heaven about things concerning our future. The easiest place to hear from God and to find God's plan for our lives is through prayer. Prayer processes the plan of God. If we will take time to pray our future out, over, down, and through, it will be much easier to walk it out!

Chapter 6
The Power of Corporate Prayer

Jesus said in Matthew 21:13, "...It is written, My house shall be called *the house of prayer*...." The house of God today is the Church—the Body of Christ.

Notice Jesus didn't say "the house of miracles, healings, teaching, preaching, or spiritual gifts." Why not? Because if we have prayer, we will have everything else.

In Matthew 12, Jesus had just driven the money-changers out of the Temple and declared His house a house of prayer. Then He said in the next verse: "And the blind and the lame came to him in the temple; and he healed them" (verse 14). When did the healing take place? When Jesus brought in reverence and made the Temple a house of prayer.

If we have prayer, we will have praise, worship, healing, signs, wonders, miracles, and prosperity. Why? Because the foundation for everything is prayer or communion with God. Prayer is what brings forth the plan of God in the Earth.

There is always an unction to pray, but in these last days there is a Churchwide unction on the Body of Christ to pray. I am beginning to understand that some things are not going to be accomplished until the Church starts praying unitedly. Until we come together like the Church did in the Book of Acts and lift our voices to God in one accord, we will not have the results they did.

It would benefit us to do a study through the Book of Acts to see the pattern the Early Church set in corporate or united prayer. We will find that every miracle and major event that took place in the Book of Acts was directly related to prayer. The majority of their prayers were united, meaning there was more than one person praying. Of course, corporate or united prayer does not replace our individual times of prayer. We will always need to keep our individual prayer lives active. Nothing can replace the fellowship and communion we have with God on a personal level every day. But we are living in a time when it is important to pray things through, and when we come together corporately, we will accomplish those things more quickly than we can any other way.

We ministered on the subject of prayer in a church not long ago. When we finished teaching, we felt it was right to have a time of corporate prayer. We all lifted our voices to God in one accord, and there was a strong unction to pray. Afterward, the pastor came to me and said, "That is the first time our church has ever done anything like that, and we are going to do it some more." I know if the Church would unite in prayer, we would begin to see more results.

"Acts 13" Meetings

When God spoke to me and said, "You're a half step behind," I knew He wasn't talking about a half step in responsibilities of the ministry. What He meant was that I was a half step behind in prayer. I reasoned that if I could be a half step or even a step behind in prayer, couldn't I also get ahead in prayer?

I want to get to the place where I have so much prayer out ahead of me, I am *walking* things out instead of *working* them out! The best way to walk things out is to get the way plowed and paved before we get there.

For the last few years, we have held what we call "Acts 13" meetings. These are meetings for ministers to come together and pray. We saw it in the Bible and thought, *If the Early Church did it, we ought to do it, too.*

> **ACTS 13:1-3**
> **1 Now there were in the church that was at Antioch certain prophets and teachers; as Barnabas, and Simeon that was called Niger, and Lucius of Cyrene, and Manaen, which had been brought up with Herod the tetrarch, and Saul.**
> **2 As they MINISTERED TO THE LORD, AND FASTED, the Holy Ghost said, Separate me Barnabas and Saul for the work whereunto I have called them.**
> **3 And WHEN THEY HAD FASTED AND PRAYED, and laid their hands on them, they sent them away.**

Verse 1 identifies several ministers who had gathered together in the church at Antioch. It seems everyone present was a minister, but if prayer will work for ministers, it will work for laymen as well.

The next verse says, "As they *ministered to the Lord,* and fasted, the Holy Ghost said...." To "minister to the Lord" means "to pray, praise, worship, and sing praises." They had all of it. This group came together with the specific purpose of getting into God's presence and seeing where God wanted to lead them. From Acts 13, it doesn't appear this was the only time the group gathered to pray. Apparently, this was a normal activity for the ministers in the Early Church.

When we saw that in the Scriptures, we decided to step out and do the same thing.

In our offices we began to hold corporate prayer meetings two to three times a year. We gathered a group of approximately 25 minister friends and prayed for two days. We started at 7 o'clock one evening and prayed until about 11 o'clock. We met again at 10 o'clock in the morning and prayed until 2:30 in the afternoon, broke for a time, came back about 7 o'clock in the evening and prayed until 10 o'clock.

Not only did we pray, but we worshipped, waited on God, moved in the gifts of the Spirit, and had a wonderful Holy Ghost time. The result of those two days of prayer caused us to catch up a half step and even go a step ahead. We still do this on a regular basis, and we have learned there is something about united prayer that causes us to catch up and get ahead more quickly than any other way.

When we come together corporately for the specific purpose of giving something to God, we make an avenue for His plans to be accomplished. We can mirror what was done in the Book of Acts and lift our voices to God in one accord. Some people walk, some kneel, and some lie down and "chew carpet." All find where they are comfortable and pray.

One thing I have noticed about corporate prayer is that when we come together, it doesn't take an hour to get through to heaven. Sometimes we accomplish the job in 10 minutes, and it's time to go home. Other times we get the job done in 10 minutes, but we want to spend the next 50 minutes basking in God's presence.

Some things are accomplished more quickly with united or corporate prayer than in any other way. Not only will things get done more quickly, but some things will not be accomplished at all unless we pray them through corporately! I don't necessarily understand why this is so, but we can see it throughout the Scriptures.

Dedication of Solomon's Temple

We noted earlier that praise is the highest kind of prayer. Praise is what the people did in Second Chronicles 5 at the dedication of Solomon's Temple.

> **2 CHRONICLES 5:13**
> **13 It came even to pass, AS THE TRUMPETERS AND SINGERS WERE AS ONE, to make ONE SOUND to be heard in PRAISING AND THANKING THE LORD; and when they lifted up their voice with the trumpets and cymbals and instruments of musick, and praised the Lord, saying, For he is good; for his mercy endureth for ever....**

What were they doing? They were ministering to the Lord in praise—the highest kind of prayer. We could say they had a corporate prayer meeting.

God may not always lead us to praise. There may be times when God wants things to be prayed through, prayed down, or prayed out. But there will also be times when we come together for a service, the power of God will come in, and we will praise the Lord for an hour and go home.

At the dedication of Solomon's Temple, the people came together and praised God corporately. What happened?

> **2 CHRONICLES 5:13,14**
> **13 ...the house was filled with a cloud, even the house of the Lord;**
> **14 So that the priests could not stand to minister by reason of the cloud: for the glory of the Lord had filled the house of God.**

Every time God puts up a new facility or moves to a new location, the first thing He does is fill it with His power. Sometimes the easiest thing to do when we have a beautiful new facility is get religious in it. It's so nice we don't want to mess anything up.

Solomon's Temple was gorgeous, and God wanted to make sure the people didn't get religious on Him. He poured out His power, knocked the priests down, and they had a Holy Ghost meeting the first night!

Jehoshaphat's Battle Plan

In Second Chronicles 20, Jehoshaphat was leading his troops into battle. He prayed, and God gave him a plan. What did God tell him to do?

> **2 CHRONICLES 20:21**
> **21 And when he had consulted with the people, HE APPOINTED SINGERS UNTO THE LORD, and that should praise the beauty of holiness, as THEY WENT OUT BEFORE THE ARMY, and to say, Praise the Lord; for his mercy endureth for ever.**

Jehoshaphat sent the praisers in before the army, and in verse 22 the Bible tells us the enemy ambushed each other! Jehoshaphat's troops never had to swing a sword.

There are things God will accomplish through united prayer and praise that won't be accomplished any other way.

Prayer in the Book of Acts

In studying the Book of Acts, we find most of the prayers were united prayers. Beginning in Acts 1, Jesus gave His disciples instructions to wait in Jerusalem until they were endued with power from on high.

ACTS 1:4,5,8
4 And, being assembled together with them,
commanded them that they should not depart
from Jerusalem, but wait for the promise of the
Father, which, saith he, ye have heard of me.
5 For John truly baptized with water; but ye
shall be baptized with the Holy Ghost not many
days hence....
8 ...But ye shall receive power, after that the Holy
Ghost is come upon you: and ye shall be witnesses
unto me both in Jerusalem, and in all Judaea, and
in Samaria, and unto the uttermost part of the
earth.

The disciples knew what God wanted to do, yet they
had never experienced the baptism of the Holy Ghost.
They didn't know what it looked like or what it felt like.
They only knew they were supposed to wait until they
received what Jesus said would change them from a
group of insecure, intimidated, timid people hiding in
an upper room into 120 bold witnesses who would
change the world. They knew enough to do what it
would take for God's power to fall. What did they do?
They prayed!

ACTS 1:13,14
13 And when they were come in, they went up into
an upper room, where abode both Peter, and
James, and John, and Andrew, Philip, and
Thomas, Bartholomew, and Matthew, James the
son of Alphaeus, and Simon Zelotes, and Judas the
brother of James.
14 THESE ALL CONTINUED WITH ONE ACCORD
IN PRAYER AND SUPPLICATION....

They came together in the Upper Room in prayer
and supplication until the Day of Pentecost suddenly
came.

> **ACTS 2:1-4**
> 1 And when the day of Pentecost was fully come, they were all with one accord in one place.
> 2 And suddenly there came a sound from heaven as of a rushing mighty wind, and it filled all the house where they were sitting.
> 3 And there appeared unto them cloven tongues like as of fire, and it sat upon each of them.
> 4 And they were all filled with the Holy Ghost, and began to speak with other tongues, as the Spirit gave them utterance.

The "suddenly" hit because they had been praying unitedly for days for the will and plan of God.

Our Own Company

In the next chapters, the disciples began to go out endued with this power to do the works of Jesus. Then, in Acts 4, Peter and John returned to their own company. Thank God for our own company! Who makes up our "own company"? The people with whom we pray. We find our own company in a place of prayer.

In Acts 4, Peter and John had been threatened by the authorities not to preach and teach in the name of Jesus.

> **ACTS 4:23-30**
> 23 And being let go, they went to their OWN COMPANY, and reported all that the chief priests and elders had said unto them.
> 24 And when they heard that, THEY LIFTED UP THEIR VOICE TO GOD IN ONE ACCORD, and said, Lord, thou art God, which hast made heaven, and earth, and the sea, and all that in them is:
> 25 Who by the mouth of thy servant David hast said, Why did the heathen rage, and the people imagine vain things?

26 The kings of the earth stood up, and the rulers were gathered together against the Lord, and against his Christ.
27 For of a truth against thy holy child Jesus, whom thou hast anointed, both Herod, and Pontius Pilate, with the Gentiles, and the people of Israel, were gathered together,
28 For to do whatsoever thy hand and thy counsel determined before to be done.
29 And now, Lord, behold their threatenings: and grant unto thy servants, that with all boldness they may speak thy word,
30 By stretching forth thine hand to heal; and that signs and wonders may be done by the name of thy holy child Jesus.

Peter and John returned to their own company and reported everything that had happened to them. The first thing they did was lift their voices in one accord—which is united prayer. They praised God, beginning in verse 24. They not only praised God; they quoted Scriptures to Him. They reminded God of what He said in His Word. The Bible says God is looking for those who will worship Him in spirit and in truth (John 4:23). God's Word is truth, and sometimes the best way to worship God is with His Word.

When they lifted their voices to God in one accord, the Church changed gears. In Acts 5, we see God doing signs and wonders through the hands of the apostles. The sick were brought on beds and couches and laid in the streets so Peter's shadow would fall on them and heal them.

Why did all this take place? God wanted to do signs and wonders, but just the fact that He wanted to do signs and wonders was not enough. The Church found out what God wanted to do; then they lifted their voices to Him in one accord and asked Him for it!

Prayer preceded everything that took place in the Book of Acts. In Acts 12, Herod had killed James with the sword and saw it pleased the people, so he took Peter into custody and was going to behead him after Easter (Acts 12:2-4).

> **ACTS 12:5,6**
> 5 Peter therefore was kept in prison: but prayer was made without ceasing of the church unto God for him.
> 6 And when Herod would have brought him forth, the same night Peter was sleeping between two soldiers, bound with two chains: and the keepers before the door kept the prison.

Peter was in prison, bound in chains, with a guard on either side of him, and probably lying on a dirt floor. He was sound asleep. Herod was going to behead him the next day, and Peter was sleeping! I love how this man entered into rest.

> **ACTS 12:7**
> 7 And, behold, the angel of the Lord came upon him, and a light shined in the prison: and he smote Peter on the side, and raised him up, saying, Arise up quickly. And his chains fell off from his hands.

I would like to think that if a light shone in from heaven and an angel walked in, I would wake up. But here was a man so totally at rest, the angel had to hit Peter to wake him up!

> **ACTS 12:8,9**
> 8 And the angel said unto him, Gird thyself, and bind on thy sandals. And so he did. And he saith unto him, Cast thy garment about thee, and follow me.
> 9 And he went out, and followed him; and wist not that it was true which was done by the angel; but thought he saw a vision.

The angel walked into the prison, hit Peter to wake him up, told him to get dressed, led him out of the prison—and then disappeared. Peter didn't know what was going on; he thought he was having a vision.

What caused this to happen? Notice what Acts 12:5 says took place when Peter was put into prison: "Peter therefore was kept in prison: but *prayer was made without ceasing of the church* unto God for him." Thank God for the local church! Thank God for our "own company."

The Church made prayer without ceasing. Sometimes we need to pray things through without ceasing. The prayer of faith will work for us individually, but sometimes for other situations we need to pray through without ceasing until we accomplish what needs to be done.

The margin of my Bible says, "Instant and earnest prayer was made by the Church." The instant and earnest prayer of the Church caused that angel to come and rescue Peter from prison. It doesn't sound like the Church spent just a few minutes praying. The Bible says:

> **ACTS 12:11-17**
> **11 And when Peter was come to himself, he said, Now I know of a surety, that the Lord hath sent his angel, and hath delivered me out of the hand of Herod, and from all the expectation of the people of the Jews.**
> **12 And when he had considered the thing, he came to the house of Mary the mother of John, whose surname was Mark; where many were gathered together praying.**
> **13 And as Peter knocked at the door of the gate, a damsel came to hearken, named Rhoda.**
> **14 And when she knew Peter's voice, she opened not the gate for gladness, but ran in, and told how Peter stood before the gate.**

15 And they said unto her, Thou art mad. But she constantly affirmed that it was even so. Then said they, It is his angel.
16 But Peter continued knocking: and when they had opened the door, and saw him, they were astonished.
17 But he, beckoning unto them with the hand to hold their peace, declared unto them how the Lord had brought him out of the prison. And he said, Go shew these things unto James, and to the brethren. And he departed, and went into another place.

The Church was still praying at the house where they had gathered to pray. When Peter arrived at the house, they didn't even believe it was him; they thought it was his angel, and they kept praying! The Church was not going to stop praying until they had results. There is something about fervent, instant, earnest prayer. We in the Church are going to learn some things about staying with it in prayer until we drag people out of the jaws of death!

Almost everything we see in the Book of Acts is connected to prayer, and usually it is united or corporate prayer. I have a bold confidence in united prayer. I know if we as a group get into the presence of God, we as a group will hear from God.

That doesn't mean we should go out and make things happen. Psalm 37:4,5 says, "Delight thyself also in the Lord; and he shall give thee the desires of thine heart. Commit thy way unto the Lord; trust also in him; and *he shall bring it to pass.*" I would rather pray it through and let God bring it to pass than pray it out one time and try to figure out how to do things myself.

Some things are not going to be accomplished in any other way but by corporate prayer. As the Church heads in this direction, we are going to pray through the mightiest move of God this Earth has ever seen: the latter rain, the harvest, and the return of the Lord Jesus to take us all home!

God is calling the Church back to a place of prayer. He is going to pull us deeper and take us higher than we have ever been before, and our prayers are going to produce more than they have ever produced before. Prayer processes the plan of God!

There is a plan of God for you, for me, and for the Church. The best thing we can do is pray it down, pray it out, pray it through, and bring God's will to pass on the Earth!

For a complete catalog of books and tape series,
or to receive Mark Brazee Ministries' free
bimonthly newsletter, please write to:

Mark Brazee Ministries
P.O. Box 1870
Broken Arrow, OK 74013